D0937117

WITHDRAWN
University of
Illinois Library
at Urbana-Champaign

ITALIAN PAINTING

in the XIVth and XVth Centuries

ITALIAN PAINTING

IN THE

XIVth and XVth Centuries

BY

GERMAIN BAZIN

ASSISTANT KEEPER OF PAINTING IN THE MUSÉE DU LOUVRE
LECTURER AT THE UNIVERSITY OF BRUSSELS

TRANSLATED FROM THE FRENCH BY

MARY CHAMOT

FRENCH AND EUROPEAN PUBLICATIONS, INC.

610, FIFTH AVENUE, NEW YORK, N. Y.

THE HYPERION PRESS, PARIS

PRINTED IN FRANCE AND BELGIUM
COPYRIGHT 1938 BY HYPERION, PARIS

8 759.5
B34Ec
cop. 2

IF a historical equivalent of the term « Renaissance » in its true sense is to be sought, it should be applied not to the XVth century, but rather to the XIth and XIIth centuries, the period when, after the long night of the dark ages, a new civilization was born. In the domain of the arts a veritable renascence took place at that time, and reached its climax in the XIIIth century; the Western renascence of plastic values, as defined by the Greeks and then submerged during seven centuries of barbarian and Oriental invasions, developing in the XIIIth century after a slow period of elaboration, which lasted about a hundred years. The principal new values, which appeared progressively in the course of this admirable evolution, which extended from the Royal Portal of Chartres to the sculpture of Rheims Cathedral, are the definite triumph of plasticity over ornament, of the human figure over the chimera, of naturalistic inspiration over the dream, a new consciousness of the three-dimentional world, signifying a return to a realistic sense of space, a new notion of artistic progress consisting of a constant approximation to life in place of the immobility of the Byzantine and pre-Romanesque arts, in which the western conquering instinct manifests itself. Thus it was France who gave the impetus to this movement, which may justly be defined by the term « Renaissance », and it was only at the moment when this brilliant creative impulse began to decline in France, that it touched Italy. In fact Italy was to accomplish in her own way a similar evolution at the end of the XIIIth century. But while in France it had been a collective effort, the product of the enthusiasm of a whole people, in Italy the individual was to play a much more important part. Many art historians, still following Vasari's estimates, look upon Cimabue as the pioneer of modern Italian art. To us, on the contrary, he appears as the last of the great Byzantines; moreover the whole of Italian painting of the XIIIth century up to Giotto is but a colony of Byzantine art flourishing in two forms : one popular and expressive in the pathetic works of the schools of Lucca and Pisa, based on the naive art born in Syria and developed in Cappadocia; the other leading towards plastic abstraction in the works of the Florentine school inspired by official tradition. The remarkably « Cimabuesque » mosaics of the Xth century, recently discovered by Mr. Whittemore in the narthex of St. Sophia, reveal that the great Cenno di Pepe drew his inspiration, probably through Venice, from the very fountain head of the official tradition, which had remained untouched by foreign contacts on the shores of the Bosphorus. The tendency to treat the figure in terms of pattern, like a playing card, consciously ignoring the third dimension and the reality of space; the deliberate desire to transmute every realistic element into an abstract scheme; to submit in this fashion every individual figure to the dignity of a general concept, susceptible to the widest extension and spiritual acceptance; all this, together with prodigious virtuosity in the treatment of linear arabesque, appears in an almost identical manner in St. Sophia and in the work of Cimabue.

This force of the Byzantine tradition in Italy during the XIIIth century accounts for the fact that the Western renascence of plastic values was delayed there by a whole century. It might have been thought that the example of Gothic art, arrived at that time to its highest development, would have shaken this tradition; and yet the art of Niccolo Pisano has its

7

roots in another and native tradition.   It is in fact remarkable that from the very beginning, the Italian school in the person of this great artist, should turn to antiquity in search of examples, realizing better than French art, the true meaning of the plastic reform.

Niccolo Pisano was Giotto's real master.   Giotto, that prodigious genius, the creator of a new world, had within him the whole future of Italian art.   He incorporated the new plastic values in a powerful synthesis with this Byzantine heritage, with which Italian art is so strongly impregnated (in a sense even Raphael may be called the last of the Byzantines).   Giotto, having discovered the three dimensions of space, asserted reality in such powerful modelling that his figures became like human megaliths.   He accepted the forms of nature, but, according to Delacroix's celebrated formula, these served him only as a dictionary.   He may have added to the vocabulary, which painters had used before, by making the dictionary undergo a cure of truth, but his syntax remained Byzantine.   He always observed the conventional hierarchy of forms, distinguishing principal from secondary objects according to moral or supernatural values, rather than according to the laws of nature, and following this law made a tree or a mountain smaller than a man.   The taste for plastic abstraction, which he inherited from Byzantium, made him subordinate his compositions to a rule that satisfied a superior harmony.   But the new, primordial, revolutionary fact is that while the Byzantine hierarchy and composition were determined by spiritual laws, here everything rests on principles of anthropocentrism.   Giotto brought the art of painting down from the ideal regions to which it had been raised by the Byzantines, and made it express the human drama.   Though he produced nothing but religious compositions and the church now claims him as one of her greatest poets, he is in reality the first man of the Renaissance to expound the Christian doctrine of grace. Giotto's figures are supermen, inwardly conscious of their own strength. The Renaissance was replacing the Christian humanism, which considered human nature as vitiated in its essence, and crippled without the adjuvant of divine grace, and man as having no appurtenance in himself, with a renewed pagan humanism and a sense of human dignity, based on the faculties of man. The saint, who raised himself above the average by means of mortifying his human nature, was now substituted by a new type of superman, who elevates himself by exalting his own nature.   The iconographic theme of the Annunciation, which brings a human being face to face with destiny, shows the difference between these two conceptions of human life particularly clearly.   Simone Martini's Virgin of the Annunciation is a poor frail creature contorted with terror at the appearance of the angel; she is the very image of human weakness.   Fra Angelico's Virgin is like a sweet and humble dove, who inclines her head and gently submits to the divine order, which fills her with grace.   Giotto's on the other hand, in the Arena chapel at Padua, is firmly planted on the earth, her head erect, and by an act of will draws forth out of herself the strength to accomplish her destiny; she is ready to face destiny on an equal footing.   Similarly St. Francis, receiving the stigmata at Assisi, is a calm and powerful hero with a robust, well-nourished body, far removed from the emaciated ascete of Mount Alverna with a mortified body and a soul prostrate by divine hypostasis, as the neo-Byzantines of the Dugento and the Sienese masters of the Trecento had depicted him. By a strange paradox there is actually nothing in painting so un-Franciscan in spirit as this immortal series of twenty-eight frescoes at Assisi, in which we witness the pathetic turns of fortune in the struggle of a hero battling against the world.

In the genesis of Italian art, Giotto is a demiurge, who creates a world by an act of will. While he was laying the foundations of all the plastic and moral values of Renaissance art in Florence, the feminine temperament of the Sienese, who always excelled in refinement, required a more substantial tradition on which it could be grafted. Duccio found this tradition in Byzantine art, Simone Martini in Gothic art. Duccio combined the two traditions, which had divided Byzantine art for centiries. He was the last of the Alexandrines. His art, derived from illumination is the supreme efflorescence of the antique grace of Alexandria, which had been piously preserved like a family tradition by the Byzantines. The angels in the Maestà at Siena have the beauty of young Hellenistic ephebes ; and the colour, with its refined, fresh tones, with its dominating accord of rosy mauve and pale sea-green, goes back in a direct line to Alexandrian painting, and the intermediate stages can be traced. From the other aspect of Byzantine art, the monastic tradition, Duccio borrowed his pathetic realism and naive sympathy, which enabled him to associate himself with human suffering, while Giotto's dramaturgy offers a spectacle regulated by a superior intelligence, from which no secret of the human heart can escape.

Duccio inflected his Alexandrian grace a little towards the Gothic manner. It was from this latter source alone that Simone derived his art. He refined upon the linear grace of Gothic art, and made it produce inflexions of a virtuosity unknown in France, which at that time was passing through a period of sterilizing mannerism. More daring than Duccio, he tackled fresco painting, and in that he revealed the shortcomings of Sienese art. Carried out on a life-size scale, his compositions look like enlarged miniatures, the figures lack solidity and float about inconsistently; one feels the absence of a close, methodic study of nature. The Sienese find nothing but picturesque accidents in nature, never the « interiora rerum », which enables the Florentines to attempt the reconstruction of the world according to definite laws; far from dominating reality, they let themselves be seduced by it. Their art, which is a cry of the heart instead of an act of the mind, suffers from all the inequalities common to whatever is based on pure emotion.

After 1340 there is a slackening of the magnificent creative effort, which marked the beginning of the XIVth century. Giotto, like Michelangelo, paralyzed Italian art for half a century. But this sudden stabilization is not due entirely to the personal influence of Giotto. The great creative movement which animated Italian art from 1260 to 1340 corresponds to the French impulse of the XIIIth century, differing in Italy owing to the causes mentioned above. Having joined and surpassed the plastic stage of the XIIIth century, Italy entered into the European rhythm. For her as for the whole of Europe the XIVth century is a period of academic art and mannerism, one of those transitional periods when after a great creative effort, the sources of human invention seem for a time to be exhausted, and the evolution of civilization remains stationary. Artists content themselves with exploiting the conquests of the preceding generation. In Italian painting we find that the Giottesque principles are gradually penetrated by the Sienese spirit in a gentle eclecticism. In Florence the Daddi and the Gaddi generations of painters guard the Giottesque heritage like a family estate, not without allowing themselves to be seduced by Sienese grace. In Siena the Lorenzetti tried to infuse something of the Florentine virile force into the anæmic spirit of Siena, but they did not understand the principle of Giotto's intellectual realism, and despite their desire for order, gave free rein to their nature and dropped into the picturesque. In Florence the enthusiasm for Giotto was so strong, that when the Cione (1) brothers tried to combat the decadence of art about 1350, they found no other salvation than in a reform, which brought back the purity of Giotto's style, based on a rational study of the master's artistic principles. Is not this a phenomenon similar to Bolognese academism though taking place two centuries before the Carracci?

The thirst for knowledge, this progressive spirit, this need for aspiration, in a word this conquering instinct which characterizes the Occidental, manifested itself in the Middle Ages in the transcendental domain. For centuries man had striven towards the supernatural world; now in the XVth century he descended to the temporal world, and nature became the object of his thirst for knowledge. At first this new passion for nature did not appear in a form hostile to the spirit of the Middle Ages; before becoming rationalized and rising against the principle of revelation, the observation of nature during the first quarter of the century was imbued with Franciscan mysticism. The artist transferred to the natural world the mystical spirit with which he had previously explored the supernatural world; he became fascinated by the « mirabilia » of the universe, as he had previously been seduced by the lives of the saints, and in his youthful enthusiasm he did not yet think of fixing the elements into scientific categories. It was in Northern Italy, in Lombardy, the ancient cisalpine Gaul, close to the mysterious forests of Gaul proper, that this taste for nature first manifested itself in a botanic and zoologic form in the works of the delightful draughtsmen and illuminators like Giovannino de' Grassi. The old chivalrous and courtly ideals, which had delighted the mediæval imagination flourished for the last time in this region, which had been so deeply impregnated by feudal civilization, and, revivified by this current of sensitive realism, gave birth to a courtly, refined and legendary art, full of gentleness, the purest expression of which appears in the work of the Veronese painters Stefano da Zevio and Pisanello. This style extended to central Italy, penetrated the Marches and Umbria, where it came into contact with another current, the old Sienese style, and this encounter produced an exquisite poet, Gentile da Fabriano.

Meanwhile in Florence the Giottesque tradition was so strong in the first quarter of the XVth century that while the sculptors Nanni di Banco, Ghiberti, Donatello announced triumphantly the great conquests of the Quattrocento, the school of painting seemed unable to throw off the tradition which was cramping its progress. Painters like Spinello Aretino, Gerini,

---

(1) Nardo, Jacopo, and Andrea di Cione; the latter known as Orcagna was the eldest, and, as painter and sculptor, was the head of the school.

Starnina, Don Lorenzo Monaco continued to apply in a gentle fashion the rules of Orcagna's reform. Some of them like Lorenzo Monaco, succeed in moving us by the sincerity with which they continue to sing the old canticles of a bygone age. But the majority can only show us a senile style. By a curious coincidence it happened to be a man of the Middle Ages, a saint, who was to found the destinies of the Florentine school of painting in the Quattrocento. The paradox is only apparent. The principles which were to revolutionize civilization appeared first within the framework of the institutions they were to destroy. Thode was right when he perceived that the sublime mysticism of St. Francis carried within it, through the principle of individualism, the ferments of Renaissance emancipation. Fra Angelico stands at the cross-roads leading from the past towards the future. One might have thought that he spent his life contemplating celestial beatitude, yet this visionary brought his sympathetic and penetrating gaze to bear upon the actual world. Like all his generation, he was moved by an ardent desire for discovery and could not remain indifferent to anything new. He created perspective with Paolo Uccello, made the conquest of modelling with Masaccio, and elaborated the rules of harmony in creating the composition of the « Sacra Conversazione », which was to have so much success in Italian art. In his marvellous evolution, deriving from Giotto, we can witness the metamorphosis of mediæval art into the art of the Renaissance. And yet the Middle Ages live on in his work. He gave life to the past for the last time in dressing it in the garb of the present. The vocation of this divine man, who might be called the conciliator, was to harmonize opposites. He united the two great tendencies, which had been so often in conflict in the Middle Ages : the theological spirit of Byzantium, acquired from the Dominicans, to whom he belonged, by which God is reached through abstract speculations ; and the spirit of Franciscan mysticism, which mounts to God by the ladder of his creatures. The faculty of reasoning, which he received from the scholastic disciples helped him in his investigation of nature, and the spirit of abstraction in his plastic speculations. All the movements of the century penetrated into his studio, but he incorporated them into his prayer. His astounding faculty of love seized only that aspect of things which unites them, not that which divides. Through love this Christian humanist reconciled the irreconcilable.

But the time of man's pride was approaching, when, keenly conscious of the faculties of understanding which distinguish him from other natural creatures, he would no longer unite with things through God, in whom all things are identified, in order to discriminate by a mental act, which conceives and objectivates. This heroic act inaugurated a new era for humanity, — the era of intelligence. It was certainly a heroic act, for it postulated the renunciation of human values, which were incompatible with reason, now proclaimed the ruling power. Disdaining the mystic sense, by which man is connected with his surroundings through a thousand links, so that he feels the pulse of the world within himself, man lost, at the same time, that intuition into the forces of the universe, which gave him a secret power over them, a power now looked upon by scientists as an actual fact. Miracles came to an end. There were to be no more miracles except scientific ones, much later, when intelligence, having reached its second stage, sought to acquire knowledge rather than power. Whatever may be said of Leonardo da Vinci, that strange man, the most universal perhaps who ever lived, and in whom all that was human was as highly developed as possible, knowledge alone satisfied the average man of the Quattrocento. Witness Leonardo himself, in whose hands painting became a *cosa mentale* and whose interest in a picture ceased as soon as it was conceived. To conceive, that is to say to bring it within himself; to make an object which can be reduced to human dimensions; to force infinity into the finite limits of human intelligence; to imprison the universal, the *ingens* within the pure geometry of thought; to submit matter to ideals, to reduce the organization of the world to an architecture based on numerical relations, — such was the dream, which intoxicated the men of the Quattrocento, who emulated their Hellenic ancestors. Refusing to submit to natural or supernatural forces, they reduced the world to nothing but a phenomenon of consciousness, aware that this consciousness is man's privilege in nature. The Quattrocento was the most heroic effort ever made to reduce the world to the measure of man. Everything converged to the horizon of human thought, like the vistas of perspective in the pictures of this period. Space itself, in which man has always seen an impression of the infinite, becomes plastic, and ceasing to be a synonym of extent becomes measurable and architectural, ordered into a perspective, which leads the eye within as rigorously as an argument. The statue, that is to say a finite enclosed space, having no connection with its surroundings, seems to be the ideal of the age; and it was the sculptors who formed the advance-guard of this movement, and were the pioneers, who broke with the Middle Ages most definitely; and the painters themselves, abandoning the qualities proper to painting, such as the modulation of values and colours, conceived their pictures as constructions in pure volume.

Masolino was the spiritual brother of Fra Angelico, with rather less saintliness and genius. Masaccio, who died at the age of twenty-seven, surpassed all the others, perhaps owing to that mysterious faculty, by which men who die young become precoursers, as though some unknown vital law required every living being to realise his destiny within the time allotted to him. A forerunner of genius, Massaccio reached in one stroke the goal, which the Italian school only attained over half a century later. Renewing Giotto's ideal of concentrated force, he preludes the XVIth century with his sense of harmonious composition, announcing Raphael; and his conception of the powerful human figure as well as his dramatic intensity recall Michelangelo. His contemporaries had not yet passed the experimental stage. They were still discovering the rules of painting, which for them were merely a problem to be solved : the conquest of spatial values, that is to say the discovery of a way of giving the illusion of three-dimensional space to the two dimensions of the picture surface. Paolo Uccello carried on this research with passionate ardour; he brought to science the naïve faith of Pisanello, and remained sensitive to the charms of nature; the dry, metallic art of Andrea del Castagno and of Domenico Veneziano on the other hand, took no account of landscape. For them the universe was a world of bronze and marble. They saw everything only from the angle of volume.

This generation of pioneers was followed by another, which does not appear to have been inspired by the same creative ardour. It found itself in a critical position.   Knowledge was identified with creation for the men of this age.   The technical process, which in the Middle Ages was considered the essence of a work of art, appeared to the Quattrocento merely an application of the creative process and this was entirely mental.   The artisan became an artist.   *Homo faber* was replaced by *Homo sapiens*.   For him everything is determined by intelligence, and perception identifies itself with conception.   Every perception becomes immediately intellectualised into a concept, nothing remains obscure in this world of thought, which is evenly illuminated like those lucid pictures filled with a clear equitable light.   The dark forces of the psychic world, which had been driven back for four centuries, were now deliberately ignored.   The man of the Quattrocento is above all a conscious creature.   He renounces sensibility as a means of understanding if it does not lend itself to the mediation of reason.   Hence the complete absence of the lyrical element in this art, except for intellectual lyricism delighting in itself, the candid lyricism, which gave the artists of this heroic generation the freshness of primitives; they were in fact the intellectual primitives.   If Delacroix sought rationally for the means of expressing passion, the men of the Quattrocento sought passionnately for the means of submitting the world to the empire of reason.

Thus the whole Quattrocento can be summed up as curiosity and energy. Man was insatiable in his desire to understand.   The possibility of exploring his intelligence seemed to him to have no limit.   Is not the only limit of a concept, a still higher concept, embracing a greater generalization?   Like the ever-widening tubes of a telescope, so these intellectual experiences become vaster and develop one from another with implacable logic and an accelerating rhythm, denoting the prodigious intellectual activity of these artistic ateliers.   However, this frenzied continuity had to come to an end. As long as the intelligence was transforming everything it touched into abstraction, it devoured the world without satiety, and was soon reduced to feeding on itself.   So long as every perception is instantly intellectualized, the lyrical effusion of the senses must be stifled at its origin; the tendency to progress essential to intellectual activity prevents the realization of harmony, which is contemplative, and requires the pitching of a tent.   The Florentines could not have heard the words of St. Peter at the Transfiguration : « Master, it is good for us to be here : if thou wilt, let us make here three tabernacles; one for thee and one for Moses and one for Elias ».

Yet the Florentines, who succeeded this generation of pioneers felt the necessity of making a halt.   Only a few, like Andrea del Verrocchio and the brothers Pollaiuolo, continued to explore fresh territory, and even they contented themselves for the most part in refining the discoveries of their predecessors.   The majority were satisfied in exploiting these acquisitions as usufructuaries.   They realised that the researches of their predecessors had attained their end, and that it was now necessary to put these conquests to constructive use.   Fra Filippo Lippi, Benozzo Gozzoli, and Ghirlandaio felt this, but as though the energy put out by the previous generation had exhausted the capital force of Florentine art, they were too feeble to face the problem.   Fra Filippo Lippi made himself agreeable, Ghirlandaio descended to bourgeois optimism, Benozzo Gozzoli undertook a scholarly

edition of Gentile da Fabriano's Franciscan poetry.   Alessio Baldovinetti
alone, with his cold rationalism approached the problem at close quarters;
the realization of perfection appeared to him, as later to Leonardo da Vinci,
attainable only by the application of rigorous laws.   His works like da
Vinci's are rare and experimental; like the master of the Gioconda he sought
the approximation of perfection in a series of closely related works, and
found it once in the Louvre Madonna, his masterpiece, and one of the masterpieces of Florentine art, a sort of pre-Gioconda.   Leonardo realized this
intellectual conception of perfection and, since it was obtained mathema-
tically, it could only be imitated henceforth.   The Gioconda brought Florentine art to a close.

After great creative epochs, two phenomena usually manifest themselves and are symptomatic of declining tension in the faculty of human
invention : academism and mannerism.   Perhaps we might consider the
facile art and aimiable eclecticism of Lippi, Pesellino, Gozzoli and Ghirlandaio as to a certain extent academic.   At the end of the century, with the
brothers Pollaiuolo, Piero di Cosimo, Sandro Botticelli, Lorenzo di Credi,
we witness the harshness, the extravagance and the *morbidezza* of mannerism.   The case of Botticelli is characteristic of the intellectual malady
rampant in Florence.   This mystical soul attracted by poetry, seduced by
harmony, found himself cursed and condemned to know no peace through
the demoniac faculty of his intelligence.   The languid melancholy of his
Madonnas, the nostalgia of his portraits, his nervous and restless style,
which gives his compositions a spasmodic rhythm, the exasperating acuity
of his line, the palpitation of his figures reveal a profound pessimism.   This
spasm is the agony of Florentine art.   Botticelli is a man who lived all
his life by intelligence alone, and in the end discovered the beauty of the
world; he tried to seize it but it was too late.   Venus, floating on her shell,
was to land on the shores of the Adriatic, not in Tuscany.

As for Siena, she was in tow of Italian art in the XVth century.   « The
winsome Sassetta lived and painted as if Florence were not forty, but forty
million miles away and as if Masaccio, Paolo Uccello and Castagno had
not yet deserted the limbo of unborn babes » writes Berenson, who clearly
saw the causes of Sienese decadence.   Having taken the path of the senses
from the start, Siena confined herself to a sentimental world, which was soon
exhausted.   She lacked the investigating force of intellect, the thirst of
knowledge, which prevented the Florentines from ever being satisfied with
the result they had attained.   Their attitude in the face of the world was
passive, they merely submitted.   But the principal defect of Sienese art
is that it was born old.   Siena never possessed a demiurge like Giotto, who
could build new traditions, but had grafted her art onto the old Byzantine
and Gothic traditions and could not detach it again.   Devoted to a religious
ideal, which their passive natures were incapable of violating, the Sienese
grew old along with it.   All that was best in the Sienese tradition passed
into the art of Fra Angelico.   Yet the first half of the century witnessed
a kind of miracle.   The pure soul of the Poverello of Assisi was born again
in Sassetta, the divine troubadour; a purer vision than his never rested upon
this world.   This phenomenon of the reappearance of a primitive style is
not isolated, and one day I hope to investigate its causes.   Sano di Pietro,

14

who succeeded Sassetta, continued it till 1481, but the lines of old age disfigured this art more and more, for all its desire to remain young. These two painters were the exceptions. The other Sienese masters, and they are numerous : Matteo di Giovanni, Neroccio, Giovanni di Paolo, Domenico di Bartolo, Girolamo di Benvenuto, Benvenuto di Giovanni, etc., obeyed the feminine temperament of Siena, which, as we already know, sought a ready made art on which to exercise their talents of refined mannerists. They found this in the art of their neighbour and former rival, Florence. They arrayed themselves with coquettish grace, like the adorable Neroccio, whose exquisite arabesque and pointed charm reminds us that the modern artist Modigliani was also a Tuscan. In some, like the fantastic Giovanni di Paolo, the old tradition of Sienese pathos, which had produced so many poignant works, died in a strangely burlesque form.

It is outside Florence, in the schools which she had emancipated, that one must look for the continuation of the great Quattrocento movement of discovery. In Umbria Piero della Francesca inherited Paolo Uccello's and Andrea del Castagno's passion for perspective, and the monumental grandeur of Masaccio. And perhaps no one has ever asserted the pride of man so haughtily as this strange man.

From its conquest of the intellectual forces, the fifteenth century derived enough pride to rise above all worldly powers, and rank on a par with divinity. We have plentiful evidence of this faith in the greatness of man. He is always represented with the arrogance of a conqueror and the haughty impassibility of a god, conscious of his strength. This pride found its fullest expression in the equestrian statue, the obsession of the century, the torment of Leonardo, the image of the human demiurge, of intellectual force dominating brutal strength. Is not the horse, as the first able organization of natural forces realised by man, the first « machine » invented by him? The sculptors were attracted by it, and certain painters too, like Uccello and Castagno. But others, like Masaccio, Piero della Francesca, and Mantegna, preferred the image of a man standing, proud of this privilege of verticality, which he alone among living beings enjoyed. Like a statue firmly planted on the ground he seems to delight in this stasis, just as mediæval man delighted in ecstasy : see Piero's Annunciation in the altarpiece at Perugia in which two statues, petrified by pride, are separated by an inviolable space. Lost in the contemplation of their own selves, these figures of Piero's are like « monads »; they would not say with the poet Keats : « When I am in a room with people, if I ever am free from speculating on creations of my own brain, then, not myself goes home to myself, but the identity of everyone in the room begins to press upon me, so that I am in a very little time annihilated. » On the contrary, the artists impose their own identity upon their surroundings. The men of the Quattrocento took up the old mediæval idea that man is « *nodus et cinculum mundi* » and nourished their proud philosophy on it. « It is a commonplace of the schools, said Pico della Mirandola, that man is a little world in which we may discern a body mingled of earthly elements, and ethereal breath, and the vegetable life of plants, and the senses of the lower animals, and reason and the intelligence of angels and a likeness to God ».

This microcosm is self-sufficient. One can understand why this proud

15

humanism was born in Italy, a country of urban civilization; for it is when man lives in town in a setting, which is itself a product of human industry, that he looks upon himself as an entity separate from nature. The rural civilization of the North, on the other hand, had produced the mystic spirit of the Middle Ages, in which man lived in close contact with nature, assisting every day at the spectacle of a thousand associations which link up all beings, and as a result conceived a superior entity in which all things are identified : God, towards whom every being must strive as to its natural end.

The Florentine school perished of anæmia for having believed in the privilege of intelligence alone, and disregarded the gifts of the imagination. And yet it came to pass that the obscure forces of the unconscious reappeared to these passionately lucid men on the edge of light and shade, round the luminous halo of the intelligence. The painters of the Quattrocento were often visited by visions of the bizarre. The burlesque *singeries* of Piero di Cosimo, the senile fidgets of Giovanni di Paolo bring us into a strange world, where we are greeted by the phantom-like impassibility of Piero della Francesca. But the schools of the North and the centre were more particularly addicted to the fantastic. The Florentine doctrines had been brought there by Tuscan sculptors like Donatello, who had come to work in Padua. The regions, which were still fascinated by the old legends of the Middle Ages, were brought into contact with this art of surveyors and geometricians without any transition. Imaginations, which for centuries had revelled in the supernatural and legendary, transformed the precise world of Florence into a chimerical universe; the school of Ferrara, with Cosimo Tura, Francesco del Cossa and Ercole de' Roberti, surpassed itself in this taste for the fantastic. The painters conceived a humanity of « flint as haughty and immobile as Pharaohs, or as convulsed with superhuman energy as the gnarled knots in the olive tree. Their claw-like hands express the manner of their contact. The architecture is piled up and baroque... The landscapes are of a world which has these many ages seen no flower or green leaf, for there is no earth, no mould, no sod, only the inhospitable rock everywhere. » (1) One can debate upon the causes of this strange phenomenon, which affected more or less the whole of Northern Italy. Mantegna is not exempt, nor even Venice. Should we see in this troubled passion a ferment of the Germanic element, which penetrated Northern Italy much more than the rest of the peninsula?

Fifteenth century Europe appears to the art historian as divided into two parts, each developing according to its own laws : the North and Italy.

The latter elaborated the values of classical humanism; and yet despite appearances, she is not quite exempt from the flamboyant baroque to which the whole of Northern Europe was subjected. The Northern provinces pay tribute to it : the flamboyant spasm of the painters of Ferrara recalls the nervous style of certain Bavarian painters. They stand in the same relation to the painters of Florence, as the Cathedral of Milan to the buildings of Michelozzo.

The impression of irreality caused by this art is cleverly produced by

---

(1) Berenson on Cosimo Tura.

16

means of surpassing the usual perception of our senses (exaggerated fore-shortening, and tactile values, impossible rocky formations, excessive relief, and disproportionate architecture). The Surrealist movement of to-day, which, by the way, has brought these strange painters back into favour, helps us to understand their neurotic psychology. The intellectual leaven created by Florence, falling into a powerful imagination, produced the greatest painter of the Quattrocento, Mantegna. He was the spiritual son of Donatello, whose living tradition he carried on in Padua. He understood all the scientific preoccupations of the Florentine painters, but enriched by their knowledge, he treated with virtuosity all these problems of foreshortening, and perspective, which they had endeavoured to solve. He added a new discovery to theirs, one which was going to be of incalculable importance. The intellectual vision of the Florentines made them perceive form, the soul of the substance, whose body is matter; for vision is the most intellectual of our senses, the one which enables us to reconstruct the world with our faculties of generalization. The operation of seeing becomes the act of conceiving, and is always more or less preceded by foresight. Mantegna, a man of the North, whose intelligence was not stifled by instinctive faculties, felt the presence of the mysterious world of matter behind form. In their investigations of the world, the Florentines had found spatial values; Mantegna discovered tactile values. He did not content himself with the visual appearance of things, he wanted to render the illusion of matter. Henceforth the painters applied themselves to the task of expressing all the varieties of matter. To Mantegna it appeared first under the aspect nearest to his geometric vision of the world : the mineral. In looking at a picture by Mantegna one can almost feel the polished surface of marbles, the coldness of metals, the hardness of corals.

Mantegna's application of all these facts of observation surpassed the experimental stage; he made a powerful synthesis of all the discoveries of the Quattrocento, and created a logical universe, rich in varied forms, with its own laws regulating the relation of objects and beings. Though belonging to another planet than ours, this universe is nevertheless complete, the beings live in their own natural surroundings. As a man of the North, Mantegna lives in close association with nature; one has only to look at the backgrounds of his pictures to see a Lilliputian world of human beings and animals seething with life, represented with perfect truth of gestures and attitudes. The man who painted the beehives of the « Agony in the Garden » at Tours is a poet sensitive to the bucolic charms of agriculture. We are far indeed from those urban painters of Florence, who lived in an abstract world, the pure creation of their minds! Mantegna is aware of the multiplicity of forms and feels their mysterious infinity; but every form he perceives with his senses is instantly subject to a strange transmutation : it becomes lapidary. Mantegna's imagination is like a petrifying source.

The Latinization, which Mantegna tried to impose upon the world he painted, contributes to project our imagination into the past. Inspired by a veritable mania for antiquity, Mantegna, together with Donatello and Alberti, was one of those who dreamed most about classical civilization. He gave form to the chimeræ of Alberti, who had dreamed of bringing the modern world back to the institutions of antiquity. No painter except

Poussin had such a sense of the poetry of history. What melancholy grandeur appears in the landscape of ruins in the Louvre St. Sebastian! Is it not possible to find the legendary atmosphere of a Pisanello in the work of Mantegna, despite all its scientific apparatus? To this man of the North, the world presents material for the imagination, not merely a region to be explored by the intelligence, like it appeared to the Florentines.

Venice, that old and prosperous Byzantine colony, remained submissive to the æsthetics of East Christian art much longer than the rest of Italy. It was not before the last quarter of the XIVth century that Venetian art began to liberate itself from the Byzantine tyranny with such painters as Lorenzo Veneziano, Caterino and Donato. In the XVth century Venice became a cross-road of influences. The Gothic and Byzantine styles, relics of the preceding age prospered there and mingled with Lombard picturesqueness and Florentine science. All this abutted in Jacopo Bellini, that astonishing artist, who has not received just recognition in the history of art because his work is so rare. But his innumerable drawings are full of the investigator's ardour; all the problems of perspective, of volume, of architecture and composition are studied in them by a man with a passion for discovery, who can yet delight in the beautiful old-world legends, and whose naïve soul is moved by the charm of nature. Jacopo Bellini is the meeting-point of the two traditions which divide Venetian painting in the Quattrocento: the pictorial tradition and the plastic tradition. They combined in him and lived on, enriched in the persons of his two sons Gentile and Giovanni, who divided them like a heritage. They had their source in the two antecedents of the Venetian school — the Gothic and Byzantine styles. Jacobello del Fiore and Michele Giambono extend a hand to Gentile Bellini, who only retained the pictorial element from his father's teaching. The splendour of Venice, the picturesqueness of her streets, animated by crowds, processions and retinues, found an ideal historiographer in Gentile, ever on the alert, with a child-like soul that everything delighted. This ingenuous lyricism was to have a long life in Venice, always more ready to enjoy than to think. Carpaccio inherited it from Gentile, and carried this spirit of another age, this spirit of faith, which marvelled at everything, the real and the imaginary, well into the XVIth century. All the old legends of the Middle Ages found their last echo in him. He still believed in knights who rescue princesses, in golden legends and miracles. But he mingled this legendary world, like a mediæval painter, with everyday reality of his native Venice, the *ombilicus mundi*, which appeared to him a suitable setting for biblical scenes and the lives of the saints. His canon of elongated proportions, his undulating and supple line, his taste for elegance, his bodies without corporeality perpetuate the Gothic style of a Pisanello, but a Pisanello possessing all the Venetian pictorial science of the early XVIth century, and the power of rendering textures and atmospheric envelopment.

The plastic tradition was more prolific. It comprised the atelier of the Vivarini of Murano, rivals of the Bellini, the Crivelli, and finally Giovanni Bellini himself and the large number of satellites who gravitated round this luminary. Like the Florentines, but more empirically, these painters were concerned with the expression of volumes; in Venice the painters also strove to win the sculptor's laurels, but with even greater exaggeration of relief, and a nervousness due perhaps to the seed of Germanic baroque latent in all the regions of Northern Italy, and particularly violent in Carlo Crivelli. All these painters produced chiefly altar-pieces, and this confined them to the single figure inscribed within its frame, in the Byzantine hieratic manner. The Vivarini, who were the last heirs of the mosaic workers of Murano, show their direct descent from Byzantine art.

What then does Venice, and Italy generally, owe to Byzantium? It was this spirit of plastic speculation, which had led the Byzantines of the Macedonian epoch like the Greeks of antiquity, to search out the canons of perfection and to give them spiritual as well as æsthetic significance; and as all perfection tends to be invariable, it was susceptible of infinite application. The progressive spirit of the Quattrocento was opposed to this conception. The contemplative ideal.proposed by Christianity reduced every activity of the human mind to the supreme state of intelligence illuminated by divine revelation; this state, once attained, arrested striving, since the end of every being was to be reabsorbed in God. Byzantine art had given the highest form to this contemplative immobility, which the Quattrocento rejected, in order that the activity of the spirit should have no limit. However, the man of the XVIth century animated, as René Huyghe said, « by a will for harmony which took the place of the will for power », rediscovered this contemplative ideal, and transported it from the transcendental to the human world, from spirituality to æsthetics. For a while art ceased to be possessed by an avidity for new conquests and contented itself in the calm enjoyment of harmony.

Nowhere does Italy's debt to Byzantium appear more clearly than in the admirable series of Madonnas by Giovanni Bellini. This had been the principal theme of Byzantine art, the one with the highest spiritual significance. Giovanni Bellini saw in it the summit of perfection, the paragon of beauty and harmony. Like Raphael at a later date, he applied himself to this theme continually in order to bring it to the greatest perfection, and reveals thereby that the aim he pursued was harmony. « Harmony, as the Greek Philosopher Philolaus said, is the unification of the multiple and the accord of the discordant ». Yet Giambellino did not reach his stage of perfection immediately. Filled with admiration for Mantegna, he first attained sculptural plasticity; seeing in each form its singularity, he insisted on articulations; but later he was fascinated by harmony, and saw what each form had in common with others, — their mutual unity. Then, instead of accentuating frontiers harshly and crudely, as Vasari says, he begins to seek out « passages ». And so the art of the XVIth century, one might even say the art of painting, was produced. Earlier art had been a matter of drawing. Giambellino abandoned sculptural values and created truly pictorial values. Making use of Mantegna's discoveries of tactile values, he delighted in the rendering of textures, but his sweet nature preferred the unctuous surface of velvets, the rustle of silks, the warmth of flesh to the hardness of marble and metal.

Two of his pictures are particularly significant, two landscapes, for this Venetian, this man of the North was sensitive to the slightest emanations of nature. The « Agony in the Garden », hanging in the National Gallery next to Mantegna's, presents the genesis of a new world. In the Bellini the atmosphere of our planet envelopes Mantegna's world of rock and lava; the landscape is the picture; the moment is approaching when man becomes intoxicated with the musical harmonies, which come to him from the universe, without bothering any longer to dissect the anatomy of nature; the figures alone remain congealed, but one can guess that they are about to awake from their long slumber of stone and be born again at the dawn which illuminates the horizon, and which is the dawn of the XVIth century.

In the Transfiguration at Naples harmony has conquered. It represents one of those landscapes of the early spring, which Bellini loved, because he knew that at that season light is more beautiful than at any other time of the year; the sky is filled with silver-nimbed clouds, one of those constructions irradiating light, that Bellini never tired of repeating, which fascinate us in nature as well as in pictures, transfixing our vision with light, and absorbing our soul in contemplation. In the middle distance a peasant is driving his oxen with a slow and peaceful rhythm. In the figures of the biblical scene there is an absence of action becoming to the subject, which, as I have said above, is the very expression of contemplation. The absence of action is characteristic of the whole of Giovanni Bellini's work, which is as static as Byzantine art. This admirable picture is, as it were, a symbol of Bellini's art. Every one of his pictures invites us to utter the words of St. Peter. to pitch our tent, and stay there indefinitely, our soul bathed in the gentle harmony it distills, and gradually fascinated by the absolute. Giovanni Bellini represents perhaps the most beautiful moment of equilibrium in Italian art. He still has the correctness, the faultless precision, the pointed arabesque, the « ostinato rigore » of the fifteenth century, and already all the harmony, and beauty of the XVIth century. His art is both architecture and music. Of all the Italian artists, he his perhaps the one who has attained the highest summit of perfection in the absolute sense of the word, with all its limitations.

Meanwhile in another region not far from Florence, another painter, Perugino elaborated the elements of ideal harmony, which was to be that of the XVIth century, while Signorelli, already haunted by Michelangelesque dreams of force and terror, carried in him the rudiments of the baroque. Bellini leads up to Giorgione and Titian, Perugino to Raphael, Signorelli to Michelangelo. The philosophy which had inspired the Quattrocento had had its day. It is to be found not so much in literary records as in works of art. In fact the Renaissance did not add much to the literary domain of human thought, though it enriched the artistic domain very considerably. Does not the mission of Italy in Western civilization consist of this prodigious gift of plastic creation, which automatically transforms thought into images and thus produces the territory of art?

THE ARTISTS

ALEMAGNA, Giovanni d', see Giovanni.

ALTICHIERO ALTICHIERI (†1395).

Plate 2.

School of Verona, born at Zevio near Verona. He painted great cycles of frescoes in Verona and, above all, in Padua with Avanzo, his regular collaborator. The historical scenes representing the *Victory of the Romans over Jugurtha* and the *Triumph of Marius*, painted in 1379 in the palace of the Podesta at Verona were an innovation in Italian art. In 1379-1380 he painted the *Life of St. James*, the *Life of St. George* and the *Martyrdom of St. Catherine* in the church of the Santo at Padua. The frescoes of St. Lucy painted by Avanzo alone in the same building show a similar style. In his war-like realism, his taste for secular subjects and portraiture, Altichiero reflects the civilization of Northern Italy, where feudalism had penetrated much more deeply than in the peninsula.

ANDREA (Bonaiuti) da Firenze. Mentioned between 1343 and 1377.

Plate 16.

Florentine painter. His principal work is the decoration of the Spanish Chapel in the cloister of Santa Maria Novella, where he painted in 1365 a great cycle of frescoes representing biblical, allegorical and historical subjects, some of which glorify the Dominican Order : (*The Triumph of Penitence, The Triumph of St. Thomas Acquinas, The History of St. Peter Martyr*). In addition to their dogmatic and iconographic importance, these frescoes are interesting in that they show very clearly the state of Florentine painting about 1350, combining Giottesque plasticity and Sienese picturesqueness in a sophisticated eclecticism. Andrea da Firenze is also the author of a *History of St. Ranieri* in the Campo Santo at Pisa.

ANGELICO, Guido di Pietro, in religion the Blessed Fra Giovanni da Fiesole (1387-1455).

Plates 23, 24, 25, I.

Florentine painter, born near Vicchio di Mugello. In 1407 he entered the Dominican convent at Fiesole, passed his novitiate at Cortona, received the name of Fra Giovanni, and returned to Fiesole. In 1409, as a result of the schism, the monks of Fiesole fled to Foligno and did not return to Fiesole till 1418. This long contact with the sweet mysticism of Umbria must have left its mark on the spirit of the young monk. The pictures of his first period from 1420 to 1430 (*Madonnas* at Frankfort, Parma, the Museo di San Marco, Florence, *Christ in Glory* in the National Gallery and the *Adoration of the Magi and Annunciation* at San Marco) show an artist who, proceeding from illumination, has assimilated both the Giottesque and the Sienese traditions in a manner recalling Lorenzo Monaco, who must have played some part in his formation. The influence of Gentile da Fabriano, who painted his *Adoration of the Magi* in Florence in 1423 is discernable in the *Adoration of the Magi* mentioned above and in the famous *Last Judgment* at San Marco. Soon after 1430 his work begins to show fresh researches into modelling, perspective, volume and the expression of spatial values, problems with which other artists were preoccupied at the time (*Madonna dei Linaiuoli*, Museum of San Marco 1433, *The Coronation of the Virgin*, Louvre, *The Descent from the Cross*, San Marco, *The Triptych* at Perugia). He begins to reproduce in his pictures the graceful architecture of Michelozzo (*Annunciation* at Cortona). In 1436 the Dominicans of Fiesole established themselves in Florence in the convent of San Marco, which Michelozzo began to reconstruct in 1437. Between 1439 and 1445 Fra Angelico decorated this convent with an admirable series of frescoes, which constitutes one of the pinnacles of Christian expression in painting. In 1445 he was called to Rome to paint frescoes in St.

Peter's, which have since disappeared. In 1447 he began the decoration of the chapel of San Brizio in the Cathedral of Orvieto, which was finished by Signorelli. Overwhelmed with work, he was assisted by his pupils Alessio Baldovinetti, Zanobi Strozzi, Benozzo Gozzoli (the thirty five panels of cupboard doors for the Annunziata were executed almost entirely by his pupils). In the frescoes in the study of Nicholas V in the Vatican (*History of St. Stephen and St. Lawrence*), which he painted in 1449, the spirit of the Renaissance already triumphs. Appointed Prior of the convent at Fiesole in 1451, he died in Rome in 1455.

ANTONELLO DA MESSINA (circa 1430?-1479).

Plates 87, 88, VIII.

Sicilian painter, and the son of a Messina sculptor. First mentioned in 1457. He came into early contact with Flemish art and learned the van Eyck technique, which enabled him to render the textures of things with an intensity previously unknown in Italian art. Some critics still admit Vasari's statement that he made a journey to Flanders. His first period, which extends up to his visit to Venice is determined by Flemish and Catalan influences (*Christ Blessing*, 1465, and *St. Jerome* in the National Gallery, *Triptych* in the Cathedral of Messina, 1473). During the second half of 1475 he was in Venice, but in November 1476 he was back in Messina. This journey was of great importance for his work, which was modified by the influence of Mantegna (*St. Sebastian*, Dresden) and probably also by that of Piero della Francesca, to whom he seems to owe the proud conception of the portrait. (*The Condottiere*, Louvre, 1475, and the male portraits at Turin and in the National Gallery, 1476). Perhaps he made a second journey to Venice, for he does not appear to show the softening influence of Giovanni Bellini until much later (*Portrait of a Man*, 1478, Berlin).

ARETINO. See SPINELLO ARETINO.

BALDOVINETTI, Alessio (1425-1499).

Plate III.

Florentine painter. He appears to have studied in the workshop of the goldsmith Finiguerra. He was also the pupil and collaborator of Fra Angelico. Having an enquiring mind, Baldovinetti devoted himself to technical researches, blending tempera with fresco and oil-painting, with the result that many of his paintings have suffered in consequence, and are very rare. He had one of the most abstract minds in Florence. His *Madonna* in the Louvre, perfect as an architectural design, is one of the masterpieces of Florentine art. The fresco representing the *Nativity* which he painted in the cloister of the Annunziata in 1463, has partly vanished, leaving only the grandly monumental contours of the figures, and a more ample landscape than had hitherto been known.

BELLINI, Gentile (1429-1507).

Plates 75, 76.

Venetian painter. The eldest son and pupil of Jacopo Bellini, he showed all his life a great affection for his natural brother Giovanni, with whom he collaborated. His first works (*Shutters of the organ of San Marco; San Lorenzo Guistiniani*, 1465, in the Accademia, Venice) reveal the influence of the sculptural art of Padua. But soon his work took a new direction. We do not know what the frescoes were that he painted from 1474 with his brother Giovanni in the Hall of the Grand Council in the Doges' Palace, as they have been destroyed. In 1749 he was sent by the Republic to Constantinople in answer to Mohamet II's request for the best painter in Venice. He brought back the *Portrait of Mohamet II* now in the National Gallery and numerous sketches, which he used in his compositions. Henceforth, Gentile was attracted by the picturesque. As an amused spectator he painted the pageantry of the streets of Venice, using as a pretext religious processions, which he had been commissioned to paint, such as the three pictures relating to the *History of the Relics of the Holy Cross*, painted from 1496-1500 for the Brotherhood of St. John the Evangelist, or the *Sermon of St. Mark at Alexandria*, which was finished by his brother Giovanni, and cleverly combines Venetian and Oriental pageantry. He painted several portraits : (*Doge Francesco Foscari*, Correr Museum, *Doge Andrea Vendramin*, Frick Collection,

New York, *Catherine Cornaro, Queen of Cyprus*, Budapest Museum.) His pupil Giovanni Mansueti continued to paint in his style till 1527, the date of his death, though he was also influenced by the younger brother Giovanni Bellini.

BELLINI, Giovanni, known as Giambellino (circa 1430-1516).

Plates 93 to 96.

Venetian painter. The most famous of a family of painters who exercised their talents in Venice in the second half of the XVth century. Natural son, pupil and collaborator of Jacopo Bellini, he was greatly influenced by Mantegna, who became his brother-in-law in 1453. He was in Padua in 1458-1460 with his brother Gentile, where Mantegna was painting the frescoes in the Eremitani chapel. He was particularly interested in the themes of the Dead Christ and the Madonna. His art became more personal between 1470-1480, and reached full expression inhis great altar-piece of *San Giobbe* (circa 1485) and the altar-piece of the *Frari* (1488) both in the Accademia in Venice; his style expanded, his compositions became richer, his subjects more varied. In 1514 he painted a *Bacchanalian scene* (Widener Collection, Philadelphia) forestalling XVIth century art. In his portraits he showed the influence of Antonello da Messina. By using an oil medium he softened with grace and harmony the harsh style of the Quattrocento, and determined the style of the XVIth century in his later work. He enjoyed a very considerable reputation, and his workshop was always much frequented. He originated an admirable school of art, which was fertile in talent : Marco Basaiti, Bartolommeo Veneto, Vincenzo Catena, Cima da Conegliano, Giovanni Mansueti, Bartolommeo Montagna, Matteo Previtali, Pier Francesco Bissolo were inspired by him. Giorgione was a pupil of his, and exercised a considerable influence on him towards the end of his life.

BELLINI, Jacobo (†1470).

Plate 69.

Venetian painter. Father of the two famous painters Giovanni and Gentile Bellini. First mentioned in 1424. He must have been a pupil of Gentile da Fabriano. He was already known about 1430-1440, as he was called to Verona (1436) and to Ferrara (1441) to the Court of the Este, where he met Pisanello and defeated him in a competition to paint the portrait of Lionello d'Este. In 1453 he married his daughter Niccolosia to Andrea Mantegna, the Paduan painter. The name of Bellini is better known through the fame of his sons than the works of the father, which have mostly disappeared or been destroyed. There are only four authentic pictures of his in existence, all identified by his signature : a *Crucifixion* in the Museum at Verona, and three *Madonnas* (Acacemmia, Venice, Brera, Milan, and Galleria Tadini Lovere). The extensive collections of drawings at the British Museum and especially in the Louvre reveals him best as the painter who emancipated Venetian art by his researches.

BOTTICELLI, Alessandro or Sandro Filipepi, known as (1444-1510).

Plates 42-45.

Florentine painter. Born and died in Florence. He was first apprenticed to a goldsmith, then entered the workshop of the painter Fra Filippo Lippi. At the beginning he was influenced by Verrocchio and Antonio Pollaiuolo in whose atelier he also worked. Unfortunately, the chronology of his pictures is rather uncertain. His first manner shows the combined influences of Lippi, Verrocchio, Pollaiuolo (*La Forza*, 1470, Uffizi; the *Madonna*, Louvre; *Judith*, Uffizi; *Saint Sebastian*, Berlin, 1473). Two of his most famous Madonnas, the *Madonna of the Magnificat*, Uffizi, and the *Madonna of the Pomegranate*, Uffizi, must be dated about 1480. In 1481-82 he painted three frescoes in the Sistine Chapel in Rome : *The Temptation of Christ, Moses and the Daughters of Jethro, The Sacrifice of Aaron's Children;* the two frescoes of the villa Lemmi, transferred to the Louvre were painted in 1485. These works show him in full maturity. About that time he painted two famous pictures of classical subjects inspired by the poems of Poliziano : *The Allegory of Spring*, Uffizi, painted perhaps before going to Rome and *The Birth of Venus*, Uffizi, which was painted after. This last work where the figure of the goddess is copied from the Medici Venus, is inspired by a poem of Poliziano in which he describes Venus Anadyomene painted by Appelles. In the same manner Botticelli attempted to reconstruct « Calumny », a lost picture by the Greek painter, from the description by Lucian. His portraits, which are rather numerous, are all stamped with deep melancholy. During the Florentine Republic 1491-1498 he was converted by the sermons of Savanarola and, in a fit of mysticism, probably burnt his pagan pictures, and began painting religious subjects with fervour (*Entombment*, Milan and Munich; *Nativity* in the National Gallery). He made a series of drawings for the Divine Comedy and these illustrations are the most beautiful plastic rendering of the poem that have ever been produced. The Pre-Raphaelite movement in England in the XIXth century was greatly inspired by Botticelli.

CARPACCIO, Vittore (†1527).

Plates 77, 78, VII.

Venetian painter. Born in Venice about 1450 of a middle-class family Scarpazza or Scarpaccia; he signed his pictures more often : *Victoris Carpathii veneti opus*. First mentioned in 1490. A pupil of Lorenzo Bastiani, he was influenced by Gentile Bellini, whose series of pictures of the Holy Cross for the Brotherhood of San Giovanni he finished. Even more than Bellini, he had a taste for great series of descriptive pictures and for the staging of pageantry, which he painted for the Brotherhoods in Venice. His principal cycles are the following : *The Legend of Saint Ursula* in nine pictures painted from 1490 to 1498 for the Confraternity of Saint Ursula; Episodes of the *Life of Saint Jerome* and *Saint George* ordered in 1502 by the Brotherhood of San Giorgio degli Schiavoni; the *Life of the Virgin* in six episodes, ordered in 1504 by the Brotherhood of Albaniano; the *History of Saint Stephen* in four pictures, now scattered, painted from 1511 to 1520 for the Brotherhood of Saint Stephen. Carpaccio's ardent imagination seizes hold of everything, architecture, trees, sea, rocks, adventures of the Saints and princesses in order to create poetry. He is one of the most sensitive landscape painters of his native town, and we have to wait for Guardi in the eighteenth century in order to find another painter so passionately devoted to the splendour of Venice.

CASTAGNO, Andrea del (1390?-1457).

Plates 36, 37.

Florentine painter. Born at Castello in the valley of Mugello. In 1442 we find him in Venice where he painted frescoes in the Chapel of San Tarasio at San Zaccaria and probably executed mosaics in the basilica of San Marco. The sojourn of this Florentine painter in Venice had a considerable influence on the development of Venetian art. In 1449 he painted the *Assumption*, now in the Berlin Museum; in 1454 he was in Rome; in 1455 he painted in semblance of relief the equestrian figure of *Niccolo Tolentino*, inspired by Paolo Uccello's *John Hawkwood*, which adjoins it in the Duomo at Florence, and based on Donatello's Gattamelata. He died of the plague in 1457, after having painted the *Last Supper* in the refectory of the hospital of Santa Maria Novella, which was his most abstract work. Andrea del Castagno belonged to the generation of painters, who tried to make painting give the illusion of sculpture; his mind was one of the most scientific and abstract in Florence. His hard, severe and haughty style reflected his suspicious and irritable character.

CIMA DA CONEGLIANO, Giovanni Battista (circa 1460-1517).

Plates 91, 92.

Venetian painter. Born at Conegliano in the Marches of Treviso. First mentioned in 1473. His earliest work is dated 1489. He was formed in Venice, where he came under the influence of Giovanni Bellini. Of all the latter's imitators he was the one who reached nearest to the master's perfection and harmony; he is distinguished among the group of Bellinesque painters for the beauty of his landscapes; but he lacked imagination and repeated the same themes and the same types throughout his life, which makes his abundant output somewhat monotonous. During the last years of his life he returned to Conegliano.

COSSA, Francesco del (1435-1477).

Painter of Ferrara. See « Ferrarese Master circa 1460 ».

COSTA, Lorenzo (circa 1460-1477).

Plate 86.

Painter of the School of the Marches. He was formed in Ferrara and was influenced by Cosimo Tura. From 1483 to 1506 he worked at Bologna. Later he entered the service of the Gonzagas of Mantua, for whom he worked until his death. At first Costa was influenced by the incantation of Tura's strong and harsh style (*The Madonna of the Bentivoglios* in the Church of San Giacomo Maggiore at Bologna, *Saint Sebastian,* Count Cassoli Collection at Reggio, Emilia). But later his style became softer and more gentle in the atmosphere of Bologna, particularly under the influence of Francia.

CRIVELLI, Carlo (1430?-died between 1493 and 1495).

Plate 79.

Venetian painter. Mentioned as active in Venice between 1444-1450. Banished from Venice in 1450, he emigrated to the Marches, where he left his best works. One can follow his progress regularly by signed and dated pictures. In 1489 he was knighted by Prince Ferdinand of Capua and placed this title with the signature on his pictures. He was influenced by the Vivarini, and carried to the extreme the Murano painters' tendency to sculptural effect. His pictures are distinguished for the splendour of their colours and the magnificence of ornament and architecture. His style is at times tormented and restless to the point of neurosis. His art was continued by Vittore Crivelli who was probably his brother and collaborator.

DOMENICO VENEZIANO. See Veneziano.

DUCCIO DI BUONINSEGNA (1260?-1319).

Plates 1, 2, 3.

Founder of the Sienese School. The date of his birth is not known, but it must have taken place about 1260. He is first mentioned in 1278. We know that this painter of Madonnas led a stormy and disordered life. It must be admitted to-day that the famous *Ruccellai Madonna* in the church of Santa Maria Novella at Florence, ascribed by Vasari to Cimabue, should be identified with a Madonna painted by Duccio for this church in 1285. The subject of the Madonna was moreover a favourite theme of Duccio's; he has treated it many times, inspired by Byzantine canons, which he softened with human tenderness. His most important work is the great altar-piece painted for the Duomo in Siena between 1308-1311 called the « *Maestà* », with the Virgin in majesty surrounded by Saints in the central panel. In the numerous panels of this altar-piece, some of which are now abroad, Duccio presents the episodes of the life of Christ with true Sienese profusion. His pathetic narrative style is directly opposed to Giotto's concentrated pathos.

ERCOLE DE ROBERTI.

Plates 84, 85.

Born between 1450 and 1460-1496. Painter of Ferrara. First mentioned in 1479. In 1480 he was in Ravenna and in 1482 at Bologna, where he worked in San Giovanni in Monte and in San Pietro. In 1486 he returned to Ferrara for good. He worked for the court of the Este till his death. Ercole de Roberti was the last of the great painters of Ferrara. He attenuated the nervous and terrible style of the Turas and Costas into a more delicate and aristocratic elegance.

FERRARESE MASTER (circa 1460).

Plate 82.

Spring forms part of a series of months painted by different masters of Ferrara. This picture which clearly shows the influence of Piero della Francesca, who came to Ferrara about 1449, has long been ascribed to Francesco del Cossa (1435-1477), author of the famous frescoes in the Schifanoia palace, Ferrara, who was, with Tura, the great painter of the school of Ferrara. But the monumental style of this work is far removed from the nervous and tormented manner of Cossa. Recently A. Venturi proposed to give this work to Galasso Galassi († 1470) another painter from Ferrara, no authentic work of whose is known to exist.

FERRARESE MASTER (circa 1480).

Plate 83.

The Family Group at Munich used to be in the Sacrati-Strozzi palace in Ferrara. It shows the haughty expression of Piero della Francesca's portraits of the Duke of Urbino. It has been attributed to Lorenzo Costa's youth (A. Venturi) or to Baldassare d'Este, both difficult to accept.

FIORENZO DI LORENZO.

Umbrian painter. See « Umbrian Master of 1473 ».

GALASSO GALASSI.

Painter of Ferrara. See « Ferrarese Master, circa 1460 ».

GENTILE DA FABRIANO (circa 1360-1427).

Plate 53.

Painter of the Marches. Born in Fabriano in the Marches. Nothing is known about the date of his birth and his youth. His great reputation caused him to be invited all over Italy. In 1408 he was in Venice, and it is probably about this time, that he painted the history of Frederick Barbarossa for the Hall of the Grand Council in the Doges' Palace. From 1414 to 1419 he was in Brescia, where he decorated a chapel for Pandolfo Malatesta. We find his name entered in the Corporation of Painters of Florence, and a year later he painted his famous *Adoration of the Magi* for the Church of the Trinity (now in the Accademia). In 1425 he was in Siena. He died in 1427 in Rome, where he was called to paint frescoes for St. John Lateran. Gentile's earliest pictures show him to have been formed in the Byzantinizing school of the Marches, continuing the style of Nuzzi, Nelli and Ghissi; later he became emancipated through contact with the picturesque realism of the North and became one of the best interpreters of poetic and chivalrous lyricism. Benozzo Gozzoli in Florence, and Pinturicchio in Perugia were inspired by him. But it was in Venice that his influence was the most prolific.

GHIRLANDAIO, Domenico Bigordi, known as del (1449-1494).

Plates 41, IV.

Florentine painter. He was formed in the workshop of Alessio Baldovinetti, but did not retain the latter's sharp style. Ghirlandaio represents, on the contrary, a relaxation in Florentine art. He seeks simple harmonies, well-ordered compositions, ample forms and gay colours; at the same time he is attracted by the picturesque, and occasionally transforms the religious scenes he paints into scenes of contemporary life. Very prolific, he painted several series of frescoes : those in the Chapel of Santa Fina, San Gimignano 1475; in the Sistine chapel, Rome; scenes from the *Life of St. Francis* in the Sassetti chapel of Santa Trinità, Florence (1485); and the *Life of the Virgin*, which includes many portraits of his contemporaries in the choir of Santa Maria Novella, Florence (1486-1490). He was greatly helped by his brother David, and by numerous pupils; he had yet another painter brother, Benedetto. His son Ridolfo also painted. His brother-in-law, Bastiano Mainardi, closely imitated his manner. Michelangelo was his pupil.

GIAMBONO, Michele.

Plate 68.

Venetian painter and worker in mosaic, he came from a family of painters in Treviso. Is regularly mentioned between 1420-1462. He was influenced by Gentile da Fabriano and Pisanello, and worked in Venice in a picturesque Northern style, not entirely renouncing Byzantinism. He made mosaics for the Mascoli Chapel in San Marco.

GIOTTINO, Maso di Banco y known as.

Plate 15.

Florentine painter working circa 1350. Several artists who imitated Giotto and were called Tommaso (diminutive Maso) have been confused under the nickname of Giottino. Modern critics tend to give that name to Maso di Banco and ascribe to him the frescoes in the Bardi chapel in Santa Croce, the *Crucifixion* in the Strozzi chapel in Santa Maria Novella, and the admirable *Pietá* in the Uffizi, in which one finds the pathetic grandeur of Giotto.

GIOTTO, Ambrogio di Bondone known as (circa 1266-1337).

Plates 11-14.

Founder of the Florentine school. Born at Colle near Vespignano in Tuscany. With the aid of numerous collaborators he executed from 1296 to 1304 a series of twenty-eight frescoes in the upper church at Assisi depicting the life of Saint Francis of Assisi. In this treatment of a new subject he gave free rein to his imagination; broke with Byzantine conventions, which still ruled Italian art, and established the foundations of Italian painting. He thus continued and completed the discoveries of his real forerunners, the sculptor Niccolo Pisano and the Roman painter Pietro Cavallini, whom he may have met in Assisi. According to one tradition, he was called to Rome in 1298 by Cardinal Stefaneschi to paint an altarpiece in St. Peter's and designed the cartoon for the mosaic of the Navicella for the atrium of this basilica. In 1305 he was sent for by Enrico Scrovegni to paint the frescoes in Santa Maria del Arena in Padua, where he met the exiled Dante. In the frescoes of the *Life of the Virgin and Christ* he attained a prodigious dramatic intensity by his method of concentration. There is perhaps nothing more nobly pathetic in painting. In the frescoes of the *History of the two St. Johns and St. Francis*, which he painted in the Bardi and Peruzzi chapels in Santa Croce, Florence, he devoted himself, on the contrary, to the research of harmonious and decorative composition. From 1311-1329 he worked chiefly in Florence. At an uncertain date, probably between 1316 and 1329, he returned to Assisi, where hep ainted the *Allegories of the Franciscan virtues* in the lower church and the frescoes for the chapel of the Magdalen. In 1326-1327 he painted frescoes in the Bargello, Florence, now almost entirely vanished, in which he introduced a portrait of Dante in the *Last Judgement*. From 1329-1331 he worked in Naples for Robert of the Two Sicilies. In 1334 he was nominated chief architect of the Duomo, Florence. He started the Campanile. Called to Avignon by Pope Benedict XII, he died before setting out, on January 8th, 1337. With the exception of his great series of frescoes, Giotto left very few paintings on panels.

GIOVANNI D'ALEMAGNA, known also as Zuan de Murano (†1450).

Plate 70.

One of many artists of German origin working in Venice. He is not well known, owing to the difficulties of identification among his compatriots of the same name, who were in Venice. He is definitely mentioned in 1441, as collaborator of his brother-in-law, Antonio Vivarini; they became inseparable until his death in 1450 at Padua, where the two painters lived since 1447. His nickname indicates, that he must have lived in Murano. These two artists' workshops produced big altar-pieces painted in richly carved framework. It is difficult to discern Giovanni's part of the work, as there is no known work by him alone.

GIOVANNI DI PAOLO (1403-1482).

Plate 52.

Sienese painter mentioned in 1423. His name is entered in the painters' guild, and he was appointed rector in 1446. He belonged to the group of Sienese neo-primitives of the XVth century. The forms of the Lorenzetti and Barna descended to him through Bartolo di Maestro Fredi and Paolo di Giovanni Fei, and became grimacing caricatures under his brush. He was under the influence of Sassetta (*Assumption* in the Collegiate Church of Asciano) of Gentile da Fabriano, and Fra Angelico, whose paradise he imitated (*Last Judgment*, Accademia, Siena). One of his strangest works is the altar-piece of *St. John the Baptist* in the Collection of Martin A. Ryerson, Chicago.

GOZZOLI, Benozzo (1424-1497).

Plate 35.

Florentine painter. Favourite pupil and collaborator of Fra Angelico; he attempted to ally the latter's angelic suavity to the picturesque lyricism of Gentile da Fabriano in a facile and rather soft style. He was a prolific decorator and painted several large series of frescoes : the series of the *Life of St. Francis* in San Francesco de Montefalco, 1450-1452; the frescoes of the *Procession of the Magi* in the Medici Chapel (now Ricardi) painted from 1459-1461, his most famous and charming work, in which he reproduced contemporary types, and which was inspired by the procession of the Byzantine Emperor John Palæologus, who attended the Council of Florence in 1439. In 1463-1467 he painted the series of the *Life of St. Augustine* in San Agostino at San Gimignano; then he went to Pisa, where he painted the series of *The Old Testament* in the Campo Santo in 1468-1485; this work is influenced by Fra Filippo Lippi and Botticelli. He also painted « cassoni ».

LIPPI, Filippino (1457-1504).

Plates 46, 47.

Florentine painter. Born at Prato, son of Filippo Lippi, who on his deathbed entrusted him to his collaborator Fra Diamante, who sent him to Botticelli. His father's influence is particularly noticeable during his first period (*The Virgin appearing to St. Bernard*, Badia, Florence, circa 1480). He was invited by the monks of the Carmine to complete Masaccio's unfinished frescoes in the Brancacci chapel and adapted himself quite naturally to the latter's monumental greatness. (End of the *History of St. Peter and St. Paul*, 1484-1485). Like Ghirlandaio, he filled his frescoes with portraits of his contemporaries. In 1489 he painted the *History of St. Thomas Aquinas* in the Church of the Minerva, Rome. During his last phase he was under the influence of Botticelli's nervous style. His compositions are awkward, agitated, his figures full of convulsive movements, his attitudes are forced (frescoes of the *Life of St. Philip and St. John*, Santa Maria Novella 1487-1502.)

LIPPI, Fra Filippo (1406-1469).

Plates II, 34.

Florentine painter. He took his vows in the Convent of the Carmelites in 1421.

He was of an independent spirit and his life is like a romance. He left the convent in 1431, and according to one tradition quoted by Vasari, he was kidnapped by Carbary pirates between 1431-1434. In 1437, while painting in a convent at Prato, he eloped with a nun, Lucrezia Buti, by whom he had a son, Filippino, who in his turn became a painter. The humanist Pope Pius II released the two delinquents from their vows, and they were then legally united. He was of an impressionable temperament and followed the general evolution of the Florentine school, without much initiative. He was first influenced by Fra Angelico and Gentile da Fabriano and painted graceful pictures (The *Virgin adoring the Child*, Berlin and Brussels, The *Annunciation*, Uffizi Gallery and San Lorenzo, Florence); about 1440 he adopted the scientist painters' preoccupation with volume (*Virgin with Saints*, in the Louvre. The *Coronation of the Virgin*, Vatican and Uffizi Gallery). In certain frescoes in the Cathedral of Prato (1457-1467) he imitated the monumental grandeur of Masaccio and tried his hand at the expression of movement, to which Botticelli was so devoted. He was one of the first to introduce a profane spirit into religious painting; he sometimes gave the Virgin and Child the features of Lucrezia Buti and Filippino. His usual collaborator, especially in Prato, was another carmelite monk, Fra Diamante.

LORENZETTI, Ambrogio (†1348).

Plates 9, 10.

Sienese painter, probably a younger brother of Pietro Lorenzetti's; he died in the same year 1348, of the black plague. First mentioned in 1319. He was formed by his brother Pietro. In 1331 he painted the frescoes in St. Francis of Siena. From 1332-1335 he worked in Florence. His most important work was the large decoration in the Hall of the Public Council in Siena painted in 1337-1339, which represents *Allegories of Good and Bad Government*. In contrast to his brother Pietro, Ambrogio assimilated Giotto's monumental plasticity, while preserving the graceful qualities of his race. The Madonna in the Seminary, Siena, is one of the most exquisite creations of Sienese art.

LORENZETTI, Pietro (†1348).

Plates 7, 8.

Sienese painter, brother of the above. First mentioned in 1305, then disappeared up to 1320, from which date he can be traced until 1348. Like his brother, he must have died of the black plague, which raged in Siena at that time. Pietro Lorenzetti was first inspired by Duccio, then became attracted by realism; from 1320 he attempted to imitate the large manner and sculptural style of Giotto. But his natural tendency towards the picturesque opposed his aim. The frescoes of the *Passion*, which he painted in the Church of St. Francis in Assisi, probably about 1340, show this contradiction. There is something of the sharp arabesque of ancient Etruria in this Sienese, devoid of grace, with hard and dry lines, a quality which was to reappear in Tuscan Quattrocento art.

LORENZO DI CREDI (1459-1537).

Florentine goldsmith and painter. In 1480 he appeared in Verrocchio's workshop, where he was a disciple of Perugino's and Leonardo's. Verrochio must have been fond of him, because in his will he commissioned him to complete the *Colleone*. The altar-piece of Pistoia, which Verrocchio was commissioned to do, is almost entirely by him. This painter followed his master's style and Leonardo's even more; he adopted the latter's feminine type and imitated his drawings, so that it is often difficult to distinguish them. A curious *Venus*, which reveals a direct study of a nude model, is almost of the same dimensions as an analogous picture by Botticelli. It has been thought that the two figures were painted for a competition for the Medici *Marine Venus*, which was won by Botticelli.

LORENZO MONACO, Pier di Giovanni, known as Don (circa 1370-1425?).

Plate 22.

Florentine painter, born in Siena, he took vows in the Camaldunese Convent of Santa Maria degli Angeli in Florence and was given the name of Don Lorenzo. He began as an illuminator and retained a very delicate sense of line and colour. Don Lorenzo Monaco continued Giotto's style, passed on to him by the Gaddi family, combining it with some Sienese grace and was more especially influenced by Simone Martini.

LORENZO VENEZIANO. See Veneziano.

MANTEGNA, Andrea (1431-1506).

Plates 72, 73, 74, VI.

Painter and engraver of Padua. Born at Isola di Cartura near Vicenza. He was adopted by a famous Paduan painter, Francesco Squarcione (1394-1474), to whom is ascribed, perhaps too generously, the reform known as « Squarcionesque », which recommended painters to imitate the antique and express relief by the study of perspective and the incisive quality of line. Yet it was after coming into contact with Donatello's sculptures in the Santo of Padua that he truly revealed his genius, and his first works, the frescoes of the history of *St. James and St. Christopher* in the Eremitani chapel, Padua (1149-1454) are in a sense a translation of Donatello's reliefs into terms of painting. It was in 1453 during the painting of these frescoes that he married Jacopo Bellini's daughter. From 1457-1459 he painted the large altar-piece of St. Zeno in Verona, the predella of which has been dispersed. In 1468 he left Padua and settled in Mantua, where he remained until his death, under the patronage of the Gonzagas and Isabella d'Este. From 1468 to 1474 he painted the decoration of the Camera degli Sposi in the Castello of Mantua showing the Gonzaga Family. He carried his studies of perspective into the vertical and executed the first illusionistic ceiling-picture. From 1484-1492 he painted for the theatre a series of cartoons, *the Triumph of Cæsar*, now at Hampton Court. During this long period of work, which lasted from 1468 until his death, he painted a large number of pictures, Madonnas, Holy Families, St. Sebastians, Adorations of the Magi, Adorations of the Shepherds etc... The large *Madonna of Victory*, ex-voto, which he painted for the Marquis of Gonzaga in 1495, is now in the Louvre. *Parnassus* and *the Triumph of Virtue* (Louvre), which he painted in 1497 for the studio of Isabella d'Este, shows the late influence of his brother-in-law Giovanni Bellini. About fifteen engravings have been attributed to Mantegna, some of which he executed himself.

MARTINI, Simone (1284?-1344).

Plates 4 to 6.

Sienese painter. Simone's painting can be divided into three periods. During the first period, which lasted from 1315 (date of his earliest known picture) to about 1330, he was a fervent admirer of Duccio's work and for that reason very Byzantine, though much influenced by Gothic art (the fresco of the *Maestà*, Palazzo Pubblico, Siena, imitated from Duccio's, is dated 1315; the polyptych, in the Museum, Pisa, 1319; the polyptych of Orvieto, 1320. During this period Simone must have travelled to Naples, perhaps in 1317, to paint an altar of St. Louis of Toulouse, now in San Lorenzo, Naples. During the second period he escaped from Byzantinism and his taste for Duccio, and allowed himself to be attracted by picturesque and profane realism. In this manner he painted the Portrait of the *Condottiere Guidoriccio dei Fogliani*, Palazzo Pubblico, Siena (1328, a fresco) and at an unknown date (circa 1325-1335?) the *History of St. Martin* in the lower church of Assisi. The works of the third period show a marked return to the graceful rendering, coupled with a certain mannerism borrowed from the Gothic, shown in the famous *Annunciation*, Uffizi Gallery (1333). The altarpiece known as the Dijon polyptych, scattered between the Louvre, Antwerp and Berlin, is reminiscent of Duccio's emotional style; he must have painted it during his sojourn at Avignon, whither he was called by Pope Benedict XII in 1339. There he met Petrarch and painted a fresco in the Cathedral of Notre Dame des Doms, now almost completely obliterated.

MASACCIO, Tommaso di Ser Giovanni di Simone Guidi, known as. (1401-1428).

Plates 27 to 30.

Florentine painter. Born at Castello San Giovanni near Florence. He was formed under Masolino as his first pictures testify (*Desco da parto* or birth plate, Berlin; *Virgin with St. Anne* in the Uffizi). The *Madonna* painted in 1426 for the Carmelites at Pisa, indicates a change of direction. A friend of the sculptors Ghiberti and Donatello, he was under the influence of sculpture and experimented in the rendering of volume. (The *Crucifixion* at Naples). In 1427 Masaccio began work in the Carmelite Church at Florence. He completed the *Expulsion* and *History of St. Peter*, which had been begun by Masolino, and had remained unfinished owing to his departure to Hungary. He attained a grandeur and power, which make these frescoes one of the principal works of the century. Their influence was to be considerable until the XVIth century.

MASOLINO DA PANICALE, Tommaso di Cristoforo Fini known as (1383-1447?).

Plate 26.

Florentine painter. Born at Panicale in the valley of the Elsa or the valley of the Arno. In 1420 he was in Rome, called there by Martin V; he painted a picture for the chapel of Santa Maria della Neve in the church of Santa Maria Maggiore, now in the Museum at Naples. The frescoes of San Clemente, Rome, (*History of St. Catherine*) seem to have been painted later, about 1430. He painted the vaults of the Collegiate church at Castiglione d'Olona in Lombardy probably soon after 1420. In 1423 he returned to Florence and in 1424 he entered the Painters' Corporation. In 1424-1425 he executed the frescoes in the Brancacci chapel at the Carmelite Church, Florence (*The Temptation, Miracle of St. Peter*), in which he reveals himself free of Giottesque influence. He interrupted his work in the Carmelite Church to go to Hungary in 1427; on his return from Hungary he painted a new series of frescoes at Castiglione d'Olona (*History of St. John the Baptist* in the Baptistery). Masolino took the step which separates the declining Giottesque style from the early Renaissance. We cannot ascribe to him the merit of having discovered this for himself. He was of a very impressionable and assimilating temperament, and his work is picturesque and graceful in Lombardy, and severe and sober, when he painted in Florence and Rome.

MELOZZO DA FORLI, Francesco. School of the Marches (1438-1494).

Plate 60.

Born at Forli in the Marches. A pupil of Piero della Francesca, whose sense of grandeur he inherited while humanising it. He was already in Rome in 1472; in 1477 he painted for Sixtus IV the *Institution of the Vatican Library*, and in 1480 the *Ascension* for the Church of the Holy Apostles, which was transferred in 1711 to the Quirinal and is now the Vatican Pinacoteca. In Rome he applied for the first time the style of illusionistic ceiling-painting, which he borrowed from Mantegna. He reached in this last work a harmonious fullness, which forecasts Raphael. Later he painted the *Liberal Arts* for the Duke of Urbino, and frescoes for the dome of the Chapel of the Treasure at Loreto.

MONTAGNA, Bartolommeo (circa 1460-1523).

Plate 90.

Painter of Vicenza. Born near Bergamo, he came to Venice in 1469. He returned to Vicenza in 1474, where he painted for several churches, and worked in Verona and Madua. Montagna was formed under the influence of Antonello da Messina, Mantegna and Alvise Vivarini. His very personal art is distinguished by a certain severe grandeur and his types are often rustic. Towards the end of his life his natural austerity was softened by Giovanni Bellini's influence. He was head of the school at Vicenza, and his style was adopted by Giovanni Buonconsiglio, known as Il Marescalco, Marcello Fogolino, and his son Benedetto Montagna.

PERUGINO, Pietro Vannuci known as (1446-1524).

Plate 64.

Umbrian painter. Born at Cittá della Pieve in Umbria. He must have learnt perspective from contact with Piero della Francesca and the mathematician Luca Paccioli, who came to Perugia in 1478. He completed his education in Florence; he worked in Verrocchio's workshop, where he was a student with Leonardo and Lorenzo di Credi. He was called to Rome in 1481 to paint frescoes in the Sistine chapel, all of which perished later with the exception of *Christ giving the Keys to St. Peter.* Back in Florence in 1486, he returned to Rome and then settled in Florence from 1491-1499, a period which was only interrupted by several journeys to the North of Italy during which, overwhelmed by commissions, he painted numerous religious pictures. In 1499 he returned to Perugia and undertook the decoration of the Cambio. The painter divided the end of his life between Perugia, Florence and Rome, continued to produce a lot of work and fell into a rapid decline. He died of the plague in 1524. Considered formerly as one of the greatest Italian mystics, Perugino's reputation has greatly decreased of late. If one appreciates the poetry of his spaces and his charm as a luminist, one cannot help criticizing him for the softness of his figures and the monotony of his compositions.

PIERO DELLA FRANCESCA, or dei Franceschi (†1492).

Plates 55 to 59.

Umbrian school. Born at Borgo San Sepolcro. He must have been formed in Florence, where he was established as Domenico Veneziano's associate in 1439. There he absorbed the Florentine spirit especially through Masaccio, Paolo Uccello and Donatello. He became councillor of Borgo San Sepolcro in 1442 and began to work there on a polyptych for the Brotherhood of the Misericordia in 1445 influenced by Sassetta, who had just finished his great polyptych, the *Life of St. Francis*, for San Sepolcro in 1444. About that time he must have got into touch with the ducal court of Urbino. About 1449 he was commissioned to paint some frescoes, now perished, at the castle of the Este in Ferrara. Probably these frescoes greatly influenced the destiny of the Ferrarese school, especially Tura and Cossa. About 1451 Piero painted the figure of *Sigismundo Pandolfo Malatesta* at the feet of St. Sigismund in the Malatesta temple at Rimini. We do not know for certain the exact dates when he was in Ancona, Pesaro and Bologna. He executed the admirable series of frescoes of *The Legend of the Cross* at San Francesco d'Arezzo, his principal work from 1452-1459. In 1459 he was called to Rome to paint in the Vatican, but he may have been there before. Only fragments of his work in Rome remain in the church of Santa Maria Maggiore. He is mentioned in a document of 1462 as living in Borgo San Sepolcro. Towards 1465 at Urbino he painted the Uffizi diptych showing the double portrait of *Federigo da Montefeltro* and of *Battista Sforza* Duke and Duchess of Urbino, one of the culminating points of his art. In 1466 he was still in Arezzo. In 1469 he went to Urbino, where he met Raphael's father. Thus he resided alternately in the two towns. In 1482 he went to Rimini. His *Nativity* in London is a late work. He died blind at Borgo San Sepolcro. Piero della Francesca is one of the highest peaks of the Quattrocento, and expressed all its monumental grandeur and pride with the greatest force. He had a scientific mind, liked perspective and geometry, and wrote two theoretical treaties : *De prospetiva pigenda* and *De quinque corporibus regularibus*; the latter was published after his death under the usurped name of his pupil the geometrician Fra Luca Paccioli.

PIERO DI COSIMO (1462-1521).

Plates 48, 49.

Florentine painter. Son of a goldsmith. A pupil of Cosimo Roselli's, whose name he took. He collaborated with him in the Sistine Chapel in 1482 and nearly the whole of the *Destruction of Pharaoh's Army in the Red Sea* is ascribed to him. It was perhaps at that time that he came into contact with Signorelli, who had a great influence on him. Of an impressionable and nervous temperament, Piero di Cosimo was successively influenced by Verrocchio, Signorelli, Botticelli. (Portrait of *Simonetta Vespucci*, Lorenzo Medici's favourite, Chantilly), then after 1495 by Lorenzo di Credi (*Portrait of a Woman*, Corsini Gallery, Rome), and finally by Leonardo da Vinci. Nervous and restless, he is in a sense a forerunner of the mannerists. The most original side of his work is perhaps seen in the painted *cassone* panels, which are mostly decorated with mythological sub-

jects, treated with a charming simplicity and humour : *Mars and Venus* (Berlin), *Death of Procris* (National Gallery), *Legend of Perseus* (Berlin and Uffizi) *Battle of the Centaurs and the Lapithae.* (National Gallery, London).

PINTURICCHIO, Bernardino di Betto known as (1454-1513).

Plate 65.

Umbrian painter. Born in Perugia. Perhaps formed under Fiorenzo di Lorenzo, he was influenced by Perugino and Benozzo Gozzoli. Like Gozzoli, he continued Gentile da Fabriano's and Pisanello's picturesque, graceful and decorative tradition of painting, but adapted it to the science of space and volume acquired by the Florentines. He left abundant works like all facile talents : two frescoes in the Sistine Chapel, in Rome, the series of the *Life of St. Bernardine* in the Church of Ara Coeli, the frescoes in the Church of Santa Maria del Popolo, and particularly the decoration of the Borgia apartments in the Vatican, executed from 1492-1494 for Pope Alexander VI. Other series of his frescoes are at Spello, and in the Cathedral Library, Siena (they were painted for Pius II from 1503-1509).

PISANELLO, Antonio (1397-1455).

Plates 67, V.

Veronese painter and medallist. Born in Verona, no doubt the son of a Pisan father. He was very likely a pupil of Stefano da Verona. He found very vivid Gothic traditions in Verona, Italy's most Northern city. A reliable document mentions him working at St. John Lateran in 1431, where he finished the frescoes begun by Gentile da Fabriano, whose influence was important for his development. His talent as animal painter, his taste for chivalrous pageantry, his knowledge of the portrait, both in painting and struck on a medal, made him very popular among the princely courts of Italy. He worked chiefly for the Este at Ferrara and the Gonzagas at Mantua. He travelled a lot, but lived in Verona. He was in Ferrara in 1435, 1438, 1442, 1444, 1448; in Mantua in 1439, 1441, 1443, 1444; in Rimini; in Milan in 1447; in Naples in 1448.

After that probably in Rome; but there is no mention of his activity after 1449. He died either in Naples or in Rome. His earliest work is the *Annunciation*, at San Fermo Maggiore, Verona, painted about 1425. The famous frescoes of St. Anastasia at Verona, representing *St. Michael* and *St. George delivering the Princess*, must have been painted between 1345 and 1438. His painted panels are very rare (the *Virgin*, Museum of Verona, *St. Eustace*, *St. George and St. Anthony*, National Gallery, portrait of a *Princess Este*, Louvre, *Lionello d'Este*, Bergamo). In 1441 he was defeated by Jacopo Bellini in a competition to paint the portrait of Lionello d'Este. The art of the medal, which he practised concurrently with painting, influenced his conception of the painted portrait. The drawings and water colours, which he accumulated, reveal a quivering sensibility, served by a prodigious virtuosity. A great number of these are in the Vallardi collection in the Louvre.

POLLAIUOLO, Antonio Benci known as (1432-1498).

Plates 38, 39.

Florentine painter, sculptor and goldsmith. He had studied with Ghiberti, Donatello and Paolo Uccello. From 1465 he usually worked with his brother Piero, who was less talented. In 1475 he painted the *Martyrdom of Saint Sebastian*, National Gallery, a work, which soon became famous. His last known painting is the *Coronation of the Virgin*, painted for the Collegiate Church of San Gimignano. As in his sculptures, Antonio the painter had a passion for incisive and sharp lines; Botticelli and Signorelli were deeply influenced by his harsh and nervous style.

SASSETTA, Stefano di Giovanni (1392-1450).

Plates 50, 51.

Sienese painter. First mentioned in 1423, he was probably a pupil of Paolo di Giovanni Fei. He was undoubtedly influenced by French illumination and was a true neo-primitive of the Quattrocento, drawing his inspiration from the Sienese tradition, Duccio, Simone, the Lorenzetti, and Barna. His most important works are : the *Nativity of the Virgin*, Ascanio, the *Adoration of the Magi* in the Chigi-Seraceni Collection, Siena, the *Procession of the Magi* in the F. Maitland Griggs collection, New-York, and particularly the big altarpiece of *St. Francis* painted for Borgo San Sepolcro (1437-1444) now divided between the Berenson Collection, the Musée Condé, Chantilly, and the National Gallery. He painted the *Temptation of St. Anthony* several times.

SIGNORELLI, Luca (circa 1450-1523).

Plates 61, 62.

Umbrian painter. Born at Cortona in Umbria. He was a pupil of Piero della Francesca and assisted him in painting the frescoes of St. Francis in Arezzo. To the influence of the latter must be added the harshness of certain Umbrian regions (the school of Foligno) and the influence of the dry, incisive, anatomical drawing of Florentine masters like the Pollaiuoli (for the latter influence see the *School of Pan*, Berlin). The monumental grandeur and impassibility of Piero must have also influenced the frescoes representing the *Angels, Prophets and Apostles* in the Basilica at Loreto, painted about 1480. In 1497 he painted nine frescoes of a series illustrating the *Life of St. Benedict* at Monte Oliveto, later finished by Sodoma; he reveals in these a remarkable study of gesture and movement, and familiar touches of realism denoting an ardent observation of life. In 1499 he was called to Orvieto to complete the frescoes of the new chapel begun by Fra Angelico. He painted the *Last Judgement* and scenes from the *Apocalypse*, the *Blessed and the Damned*. Here he gave free play to his passionate temperament, painting the contortions of frenzied bodies, in violently dramatic compositions in a trenchant and nervous style, dissecting muscles as in an anatomical plate and agitating the bodies with frantic convulsions. This terrible vision, revealing the admitted influence of Dante, anticipates the work of Michelangelo in the Sistine Chapel. Animated by a passionate creative energy, Signorelli has left a large number of other pictures.

SIMONE MARTINI. See Martini.

SPINELLO. Aretino (†1410).

Plate 18.

Florentine painter. Born at Arezzo, a pupil of Agnolo Gaddi. He worked in Florence, Pisa, Lucca, Arezzo. He was one of the late Giottesques, who carried on the traditions of the founder of the Florentine school up to the dawn of the XVth century. He painted series of rather monotonous frescoes (*History of St. Ephesius*, Campo Santo, Pisa 1391-92; *The Wars of Frederick Barbarossa and Alexander III*, Palazzo Pubblico, Siena, 1408-1410). He was assisted by his son and disciple Parri Spinelli.

STEFANO DA VERONA, often wrongly known as da Zevio (circa 1375-1451).

Plate 66.

Veronese painter. He lived in the region of Trent. His works are limited to a few paintings on panels (*Virgin*, Colonna Gallery, Rome; *Adoration of the Magi*, Brera Gallery, Milan; *Virgin with Angels* at Illasi). His delicate art surpasses even Pisanello's in refinement, if not in elegance. He proceeds from the Gothic style, and was profoundly influenced by the Rhenish painters, as is shown in the two pictures of the *Virgin in the Garden*, Museum of Verona and Worcester Museum. It seeems he exercised a great influence in the North of Italy. He died in Trent.

TOMMASO DA MODENA (†1379).

Plate 19.

Modenese painter, who worked in Modena and Treviso. Influenced by Giotto, he was nevertheless one of the most personal painters of the Trecento. Of a violent disposition he carried the expression of realism to the point of naturalism (series of the *Dominican Doctors* in the chapter-house of the Dominicans of Treviso, 1352) and manifested a passionate taste for pathos (*Life of St. Ursula*, Museum of Treviso). He was invited by Charles IV to work in the Castle of Karlstein, a journey, which had a great influence on the origin of the Czech school of painting.

TRAINI, Francesco.

Plate 170.

Painter of Pisa. First mentioned in 1322 till 1364. There exist two authentic works of this painter, an altar-piece of the *Life of St. Dominic* (Museum and Seminary, Pisa) painted 1344, and a *Triumph of St. Thomas Aquinas* in the Cathedral, Pisa. The Lorenzetti's influence is manifest in these works; and it is for this reason that a large series of frescoes in the Campo Santo of Pisa, so important for the iconography of the Middle Ages, and so like the Lorenzetti manner, is ascribed to him (*The Life of the Hermits, The Triumph of Death, The Quick and the Dead* and *The Last Judgment*). However, this supposition is uncertain.

TURA Cosimo or Cosmè (1430-1495).

Plates 80, 81.

Ferrarese painter. He was influenced by Pietro della Francesca, who came in 1449 to paint frescoes at the Este palace, and by Mantegna, whose style was revealed in the chapel of the Eremitani in Padua from 1448-1454. He was mentioned in Ferrara in 1451 and 1452. Later he went to Padua and Venice, where he remained until 1457. The following years he worked for the Este family. He probably decorated the library of Pico de la Mirandola between 1465 and 1467 and then returned for good to Ferrara, where he worked for the Este until his death. Nervous and tormented and inclined towards the fantastic, he is the strangest painter of the Quattrocento.

UCCELLO, Paolo di Dono, known as (1396?-1475).

Plate 31.

Florentine goldsmith and painter. He began by working with Ghiberti on the second door of the Baptistery, Florence. He was also a friend of Donatello's. His education as sculptor explains the passionate taste for seeking to express volume in painting. He was in Venice from 1425 to 1432, where he worked

34

on the façade of St. Mark's. He returned to Florence in 1433. In 1336 he painted an equestrian figure of the *Condottiere John Hawkwood* in the Duomo, a work in which he seeks to give an illusion of sculpture; this figure seems to have inspired Donatello's conception of his Gattamelata. He painted three pictures of battles for the Medici palace (now in the Uffizi, the Louvre and the National Gallery) where he essayed an audacious foreshortening of volumes. In them as well as in his *Hunt* in the Oxford Museum, he imitated the French « verdures » tapestries, for this painter, who was in love with scientific realism, remained susceptible to Northern lyricism. From 1440-1450 he executed the frescoes of the Chiostro Verde, Santa Maria Novella, in monochrome painting, his most masterly work, unfortunately much deteriorated, showing his application to the study of perspective, which he passionately loved. From 1455-1458 he painted an altar-piece for the Corpus Domini of Urbino, of which only the predella remains, a work revealing his lyrical tendency. Uccello's painting charms one by the ardent beauty of its colour, which is an exception in the Florentine School.

UMBRIAN MASTER (of 1473).

Plate 63.

The picture representing the birth of St. Bernardine forms part of a series of eight panels painted in 1473 and kept in the Pinacoteca, Perugia; they probably adorned a large shrine, which was destined to enclose the banner of St. Bernardine. This work, in which the grandeur of architecture clearly reveals Piero della Francesca's influence, is one of the masterpieces of Umbrian art. The elegance of the figures announces Perugino's and Pinturicchio's styles. but with something more nervous. For a long time it had been ascribed to Fiorenzo di Lorenzo (circa 1440-died between 1522 and 1525) a Perugian master, whose style proceeds from the dry manner of Alunno and who is very far from the linear elegance of the St. Bernardine panels. Several hands can be distinguished in this work. Berenson suggests the names of Perugino, Bonfigli and Caporali. I am inclined to agree with Van Marle who, tentatively ascribes at least one of the panels (4) to

a special master, « the master of 1473 ». He gives two other panels to Pinturicchio and the two last, more mediocre ones to an « assistant of the Master of 1473 ».

VENEZIANO, Dominico (†1461).

Plates 32, 33.

Painter of Venetian origin, who painted in Florence. First mentioned in 1438 at Perugia, but in 1439 he was in Florence working for the Medici. We know that he used an oil medium. Vasari makes him out to be the hero of a melodrama, which the critics have disproved, and which forms a part of what might be called « the romance of oil-painting ». He was supposed to have been murdered by Andrea del Castagno, who wanted to steal from him the secret of painting in oils. But the murdered man lived four years longer than his assassin. He was influenced by the scientific generation of Florentine painters and sculptors, but brought a certain Venetian softness to the Florentine rigour, and his tender colouring contrasted unpleasantly with the severe harmonies of Florentine art. He was the master of Piero della Francesca and Baldovinetti.

VENEZIANO, Lorenzo.

Plate 21.

Venetian painter mentioned between 1357 and 1372. No details of his biography are known, but he left a certain number of signed and dated pictures. (At the Accademia, Venice : a large altar-piece of the *Annunciation*, 1357: the *Marriage of St. Catherine*, 1358; the *Annunciation*, 1371; a *Madonna* at the Louvre 1372, etc.). Lorenzo Veneziano played a leading part in the Venetian school. He gave a definite impulse to a movement of liberation from Byzantinism begun by Maestro Paolo. The influence of Gothic art helped him to emancipate himself from the Byzantine canons.

VERROCCHIO, Andrea di Cione known as del (1435-1488).

Plate 63.

Florentine painter, goldsmith and sculptor. He was a pupil of Verrocchio the goldsmith, whose name he adopted. He spent all his life in Florence until the day he was called to Venice in 1483 to execute the statue of *Colleone*; he died in Venice in 1488. His works as a painter are not numerous : the *Annunciation* of the Uffizi is sometimes ascribed to Leonardo; the *Madonna* of the Duomo, Pistoia, was almost entirely the work of Lorenzo di Credi; in the *Baptism of Christ* in the Accademia, Florence, the dry modelling of St. John the Baptist and the admirable anatomy of Christ reveal the sculptor; according to Vasari the graceful angel on the left and the misty landscape in the back ground are by Leonardo, who was a pupil of Verrocchio's.

VIVARINI, Alvise (circa 1464-1503).

Plate 89.

Venetian painter. He was the last of a dynasty of artists from Murano, whose workshop rivalled Bellini's in the XVth century. He was a pupil and collaborator of his father Antonio, and his uncle Bartolommeo and at first continued their harsh and severe style; but he was influenced by Giovanni Bellini and Antonello da Messina and modernised the methods of his workshop, without ever reaching the quality of Giovanni's art. He painted exclusively religious pictures with the exception of a few portraits.

VIVARINI, Antonio, (known as Antonio da Murano).

Plate 70.

Venetian painter. Mentioned between 1435 and 1476. Born of a family of painters and mosaicists working in Murano, near Venice, where Byzantine traditions were kept very pure until the XVth century, he worked in Venice, Parenzo, Milan, Padua. From 1441 to 1449 he often collaborated with Giovanni d'Alemagna, a German painter established in Venice, and from 1450 with his brother Bartolommeo Vivarini. Antonio Vivarini was influenced by Gentile da Fabriano and Pisanello and combined the Northern Gothic style with a hieratic manner, which he drew from Byzantine art, and had already a certain inclination to the study of volume. His Venetian temperament loved the beauty of subject and richness of ornament.

VIVARINI, Bartolommeo (circa 1431-1499).

Plate 71.

Venetian painter. At first a pupil and collaborator of his brother Antonio. The art of Bartolommeo Vivarini differs from that of his brother in his passionate desire to express volume by exaggerated relief and sharpness of drawing, but he had the same taste for ornamental magnificence.

BIBLIOGRAPHY

Giorgio VASARI : Le Vite dé piu eccellenti Architetti, Pittori e Scultori Italiani, Florence, 1550, 2nd edition, Florence, 1568; C. Milanesi edit., Florence, 1878-1881 (9 vol.). — Luigi LANZI : Storia Pittorica della Italia, Milan, 1824-1825 (4 vol.). — Jacob BURKHARDT : Der Cicerone, Basle, 1855; 10th edition directed by W. Bode, Leipzig, 1910; French translation by Gérard, Paris, 1892. — ID. : Die Kultur der Renaissance in Italien, 1860; Goldscheider edit., illustr., Vienna, 1935; French edit. by Schmitt : La civilisation en Italie au temps de la Renaissance, Paris, 1877. — I. A. CROWE and G. B. CALVACASELLE : A new History of Painting in Italy, London, 1864-1866; Langton Douglas edit., London, 1903-1914 (6 vol.). — ID. : A History of Painting in North Italy; edit. by T. Borenius, London, 1912 (3 vol.). — H. TAINE : Voyage en Italie, 2 vol., Paris, 1866. — G. LAFENESTRE : La Peinture Italienne depuis les origines jusqu'à la fin du xve siècle, Paris, 1885. — E. MUNTZ : Histoire de l'art pendant la Renaissance, 3 vol., Paris, 1889-1891, completed Italian edition, Florence, 1902. — Ivan LERMOLIEFF : (Gio Morelli), Kunstkritische Studien, Leipzig, 1890-1898 (3 vol.). — H. BRANDI : Die Renaissance in Florenz und Rom, Leipzig, 1900. — Ad. VENTURI : Storia dell'Arte Italiana, Milan, 1901 (22 vol. issued). — B. BERENSON : The Study and Criticism of Art, London, 1901-1916 (3 vol.). — ID. : Italian Painters of the Renaissance, Oxford, 1930, 2nd edition in French, illustr., Paris, 1937. — ID. : Italian Pictures of the Renaissance (Catalogue), Oxford, 1932, 2nd edition in Italian : Pitture italiana del Rinascimento, catalogo dei principali artisti e dello loro opere), Milan, 1936. — PERATE : La peinture italienne (des origines au xvie siècle), in André MICHEL'S Histoire de l'art depuis les premiers temps chrétiens jusqu'à nos jours, vol. II, part. I, pp. 421-458 (1906), part II, pp. 777-970 (1907); vol. III, part. II, pp. 589-742 (1908); vol. IV, part. I, pp. 245-490 (1909). — W. V. BODE : Die Kunst der Früherenaissance, Berlin, 1923 (Propylaen-Kunstgeschichte). — R. VAN MARLE : The Development of the Italian Schools of Painting, The Hague, 1923-1926 (18 vol.). — Louis HAUTECŒUR : Les primitifs italiens, Paris, 1931. — René HUYGHE : L'art italien au xiiie et xive siècles, L'art italien au xve siècle, in Léon DESHAIRS'S : L'art des origines à nos jours, Paris, 1932, vol. II, pp. 241-276. — ID. : Peinture italienne, 2 vol., 1935. — L. VENTURI : Italian Paintings in America, New-York, Milan, 1933. — U. OJETTI : Atlante, di storia dell'arte italiana, 2 vol., Milan, 1934. — V. THIEME and F. BECKER : Allgemeines Künstlerlexikon, Leipzig, 1901, passim.

Florence : G. SOULIER : Les influences orientales dans la peinture toscane, Paris, 1924. P. TOESCA : Die Florentinische Malerei des 14 Jahrh., Munich-Florence, 1929. O. G. GIGLIOLI : Toscana, Bergamo, 1932. R. OFFNER : A Critical and Historical Corpus of Florentine Painting, New-York (5 vol. issued since 1930). Abel LETALLE : Les fresques du Campo-Santo de Pise, Paris, undated. Mostra Giottesca (Catalogue), Bergamo, 1937. — Siena : E. JACOBSEN : Sienesische Meister des Trecento, Strasbrug, 1907. ID. : Das Quattrocento in Siena, Strasburg, 1908. E. CECCHI : Trecentisti Senesi, Rome, 1928. G. H. WEIGELT : Die Sienesische Malerei des 14 Jahrh., Florence, Munich, 1930. Louis GIELLY : Les primitifs siennois, Paris, undated. — Umbria : E. JACOBSEN : Umbrische Malerei, Strasburg, 1914. W. BOMBE : Geschichte der Peruginer Malerei, Berlin, 1912. — The Marches : A. COLASSANTI : Die Malerei des 15 Jahrh. in den italienischen Marksen, Berlin-Florence, 1934. Luigi SERRA : L'Arte delle Marche, Rome, 1934. — Emilia : Ad. VENTURI : Die Malerei des 15 Jahrh. in der Emilia (Bologna and Ferrara), Berlin-Florence, 1931. R. LONGHI : Officina ferrarese, Rome, 1934. Catalogo della Esposizione delle Pittura ferrarese del Rinascimento, Ferrara, 1933. — Northern Italy : P. TOESCA : La pitture e la miniature nella Lombardia, Milan, 1912. Ad. VENTURI : Die Malerei des 15 Jahrh. in Oberitalien (Lombardy, Piedmont, Liguria), Berlin-Florence, 1930. — Venetia : C. RIDOLFI : Le Maraviglie dell'Arte, Venice, 1648; Hadeln ed., Berlin, 1914-1924 (2 vol.). T. BORENIUS : The Painters of Vincenza, London, 1909. J.-L. VENTURA : Le origini della Pittura veneziana, Venice, 1907. Laud. TESTI : Storia della Pittura Veneziana, Bergamo, 1909-1915 (2 vol.).

Altlchlero : L. BRONSTEIN : A l'artiste et son œuvre, Paris, 1932. — Fra Angelico : Fr. SCHOTTMULLER . F. A. da Fiesole (Klassiker der Kunst, 2nd ed., Stuttgart, 1924. A. PICHON : F. A., Paris, undated. E. SCHNEIDER : F. A. da Fiesole, Paris 1933. — The Bellini : E. CAMMAERTS : Les B., Paris, undated.. G. GRONAU : Giovanni B. (Klassiker der Kunst), Leipzig, 1930. L. DUSSLER : Giovanni B., Frankfort, 1935. — Botticelli : H. P. HORNE : A. Filipepi, commonly called Sandro Botticelli, London, 1908. W. V BODE : S. B. (Klassiker der Kunst), Stuttgart 1926. R. SCHNEIDER : S.B. Paris, undated. C. DIEHL : Botticelli, Paris, undated. M. BRION : B., Paris, 1931. G. GAMBA : B., Paris, 1937. L. VENTURI : S. B., Paris-Vienna, 1937. — Carpaccio : G. FIOCCO : C., Paris-Rome, 1931. G. and L. ROSENTHAL : C., Paris, undated, G. LUDWIG and P. MOLMENTI : V. C., sa vie, ses œuvres, son temps, Paris, 1910. — Cima : R. BURCKHART : C. da Conegliano, Leipzig, 1905. — Crivelli : F. DREY : C., Munich, 1927. — Duccio : C. H. WEIGELT : D. di Buoninsegna, Leipzig, 1911. — Fiorenzo di Lorenzo : S. WEBER : F. di L., Strasburg, 1904. — Foppa : J. FFOULKES and R. MAIOCCHI : V. F., London and New-York, 1909. — Gentile da Fabriano : A. COLASANTI : G. da F. (Bergamo), 1909. — Ghirlandaio : H. HAUVETTE : D. G., Paris, 1908. P. E. KUPPERS : Die Tafelbilder des D. G., Strasburg, 1906. — Giotto : O. SIREN : G. and some of his Followers, Cambridge, 1917. C. H. WEIGELT : G. (Klassiker der Kunst), Stuttgart, 1925. C. BAYET : G., Paris, undated. M. BRION : G., Paris, undated. L. GIELLY : G., Paris, 1931. J. ALAZARD : G., Paris, 1937. — Giovanni di Paolo : Cesare BRANDI : G. di P., Siena. — Gozzoli : U. MENGIN : B. G., Paris, 1909. G. J. HOOGEWERF : B. G., Paris, 1930. E. GONTALDI : B. G., Milan, 1928. M. LAGAISSE : B. G., Paris, 1934. — The Lippi : I. B. SUPPINO : Les deux L., Florence, 1904. U. MENGIN : Les deux L., Paris, 1932. H. MENDELSSOHN : Filippo L., Berlin, 1909. A. SCHARF : Filippino Lippi, Vienna, 1935. — Lorenzo Monaco : V. GOLZIO : L. M., Rome, 1931. — The Lorenzetti : G. SINIBALDI : I. L., Florence, 1933. E. CECCHI : Pietro L., Milan, 1930. — Mantegna : C. YRIARTE : M., sa vie, sa maison, son tombeau, ses œuvres, Paris, 1901. F. KNAPP : A. M. (Klassiker der Kunst), Leipzig, 1924, French edition (after the first German edition, Paris, 1911, without the name of the author). G. FIOCCO : L'arte di A. M., Bologna, 1927. A. BLUM : A., Paris, undated. — Masaccio and Masolino : A. SCHMARSOW : Masolino and Masaccio, Leipzig, 1928. H. LINDBERG : To the Problem of Masolino and Masaccio, Stockholm, 1931. J. MESNIL : Masaccio et les débuts de la Renaissance, The Hague, 1927, M. SALMI : Masaccio, Rome, 1932. M. PITTALUGA : Masaccio, Florence, 1935. — Perugino : W. BOMBE : P. (Klassiker der Kunst), Stuttgart, 1914. F. CANUTI : P., 2 vol., Siena, undated. J. ALAZARD : P., Paris, 1927. — Piero di Cosimo : F. KNAPP : P. di C., Halle, 1898. — Piero della Francesca : H. GRABER : P. d. F., Basle, 1920. R. LONGHI : P. d. F., Paris, 1927. — Pinturicchio : C. RICCI : Il P., Perugia, 1912. A. GOFIN : P., Paris, undated. — Pisanello : Les dessins de P. et de son école conservés au Musée du Louvre, 3 vol. in-folio, Paris, 1911. J. DE FOVILLE : P. et les médailleurs italiens, Paris, undated. A. CALARI and O. CORNAGGIA : P., Milan, 1928. A. H. MARTINIE : P., Paris, 1930. J. BABELON : P., Paris, 1930. — The Pollaiuoili : M. Cruttwell : Antonio and Piero P., London, 1907. — Sassetta : B. BERENSON : A Sienese Painter of the Franciscan Legend, London, 1909. — Signorelli : L. DUSSLER : L. S. (Klassiker der Kunst), Stuttgart, 1927. — Simone Martini : R. VAN MARLE : S. M., Strasburg, 1920. — Spinello Aretino : G. GOMBOSI : S. A., Budapest, 1926. — Tommaso da Modena : L. COLETTI : L'Arte di T. da M., Bologna, 1933. — Uccello : Ph. SOUPAULT : P. U., Paris, 1929. — Verrocchio : M. CRUTTWELL : V., London, 1904. M. REYMOND : V., Paris, undated. — The Vivarini : G. SINIGAGLIA : De Vivarini, Bergamo, 1905.

PRINTED IN BELGIUM

THE WORKS

1

DUCCIO DI BUONINSEGNA

Madonna with Angels
(« Rucellai Madonna »)
1285
Cappella Rucellai, Santa Maria Novella,
Florence.

2

DUCCIO DI BUONINSEGNA

Christ on the Mount of Olives, reverse of
  the Maestà
1308-1311
Opera del Duomo, Siena.

3

DUCCIO DI BUONINSEGNA

The Temptation of Christ, from the Maestà
    altar-piece
1308-1311
H. C. Frick Collection, New-York.

4

SIMONE MARTINI

St. Louis of Toulouse Enthroned. crowning
his Brother Robert of Anjou
1317
Museo Nazionale, Naples.

5

SIMONE MARTINI

St. Martin before the Emperor
St. Francesco, Chapel of St. Martin, Assisi.

6

SIMONE MARTINI and LIPPO
MEMMI

Annunciation
1333
Galleria degli Uffizi, Florence.

7

PIETRO LORENZETTI

Descent from the Cross
St. Francesco, Assisi.

8

PIETRO LORENZETTI

Birth of the Virgin
1342.
Opera del Duomo, Siena.

9

AMBROGIO LORENZETTI

Good Government (detail)
1338-1339
Palazzo Pubblico, Sala della Pace, Siena.

10

AMBROGIO LORENZETTI

Madonna nursing Child
Seminario Arcivescovile, Chapel, Siena.

11

GIOTTO DI BONDONE

The Flight into Egypt
1303-1306
Arena Chapel, Padua.

12

GIOTTO DI BONDONE

Christ Appearing to Mary Magdalen
1303-1306
Arena Chapel, Padua.

GIOTTO DI BONDONE

Madonna Enthroned and Angels
Galleria degli Uffizi, Florence.

13

14

GIOTTO DI BONDONE

Death of St. Francis of Assisi
Santa Croce, Bardi Chapel, Florence.

15

MASO DI BANCO known as GIOTTINO

Descent from the Cross
Galleria degli Uffizi, Florence.

16

ANDREA DA FIRENZE

The Church Triumphant (detail)
Spanish Chapel, Santa Maria Novella,
Florence.

17

FRANCESCO TRAINI

The Triumph of Death
Campo Santo, Pisa.

18

SPINELLO ARETINO

Frederick Barbarossa and Doge Sebastiano Ziani accompanying Pope Alexander III to Rome (detail)
1408-1410
Sala di Balia, Palazzo Pubblico, Siena.

19

TOMMASO DA MODENA

Fra Giovanni da Schio
1352
Chapter House, Convent of the
Dominican Order, Treviso.

ALTICHIERO

Crucifixion
Oratorio di S. Giorgio, Padua.

21

LORENZO   VENEZIANO

The Virgin and Child
1372
Musée du Louvre, Paris.

23

FRA ANGELICO DA FIESOLE

Descent from the Cross
Museo di S. Marco, Florence.

24

FRA ANGELICO DA FIESOLE

Annunciation
Convent of S. Marco, Florence.

25

FRA ANGELICO DA FIESOLE

St. Laurence distributing Alms
Chapel of Nicholas V, Vatican, Rome.

I

FRA ANGELICO DA FIESOLE

Coronation of the Virgin
Circa 1425-1430
Musée du Louvre, Paris.

Fra GIOVANNI DA FIESOLE dit L'ANGÉLICO
Le Couronnement de la Vierge

MASOLINO DA PANICALE

Salome presenting Herodias with the
Head of St. John the Baptist.
Collegiata Baptistery, Castiglione d'Olona.

27

MASACCIO

Tribute Money
Brancacci Chapel. Carmine, Florence.

28

MASACCIO

St. Peter healing the Sick
Brancacci Chapel, Carmine, Florence.

29

MASACCIO
Crucifixion
1426
Musco Nazionale, Naples.

30

MASACCIO

Adoration of the Magi
(Predella of the Altar of Pisa)
1426
Kaiser Friedrich Museum, Berlin.

31

PAOLO UCCELLO

Battle of S. Romano
Galleria degli Uffizi, Florence.

32

DOMENICO VENEZIANO

Madonna and four Saints
Galleria degli Uffizi, Florence.

33

DOMENICO VENEZIANO

Portrait of a Young Woman
Kaiser Friedrich Museum, Berlin.

34

FRA FILIPPO LIPPI

The Dance of Salome
Chapel of the Choir, Prato Cathedral.

II

FRA FILIPPO LIPPI

Madonna and two Saints
1437
Musée du Louvre, Paris.

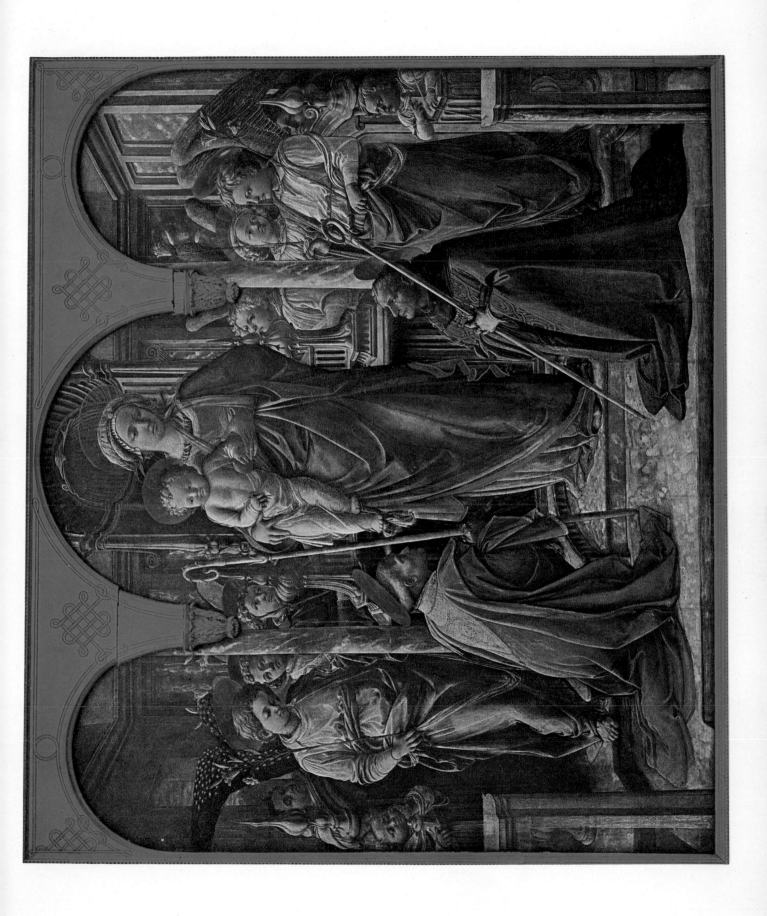

35

BENOZZO GOZZOLI

Procession of the Magi (detail)
1459
Palazzo Riccardi, Florence.

36

ANDREA DEL CASTAGNO

The Last Supper
Castagno Museum (S. Apollonia), Florence.

37

ANDREA DEL CASTAGNO

Portrait of a Florentine
Andrew Mellon Collection, Washington D.C.

III

ALESSIO BALDOVINETTI

Madonna in a Landscape
Musée du Louvre, Paris.

38

ANTONIO DEL POLLAIJOLO

Tobias and the Angel
Royal Pinacotheca, Turin.

39

ANTONIO DEL POLLAIUOLO

Rape of Dejanira
Yale University, New Haven.

40

ANDREA DEL VERROCCHIO

The Baptism of Christ
Galleria degli Uffizi, Florence.

ARS VTINAM MORES
ANIMVM QVE EFFINGERE
POSSES PVLCHRIOR IN TER
RIS NVLLA TABELLA FORET
MCCCCLXXXVIII

41

DOMENICO GHIRLANDAIO

Portrait of Giovanna Albizzi Tornabuoni
1488
Edsel Ford Collection, Detroit, U.S.A.

IV

DOMENICO GHIRLANDAIO

The Visitation
1491
Musée du Louvre, Paris.

42

SANDRO·BOTTICELLI

Madonna with Angels
Kaiser Friedrich Museum, Berlin.

43

SANDRO BOTTICELLI

Primavera
Galleria degli Uffizi, Florence.

44

SANDRO BOTTICELLI

Portrait of a Young Man
National Gallery, London.

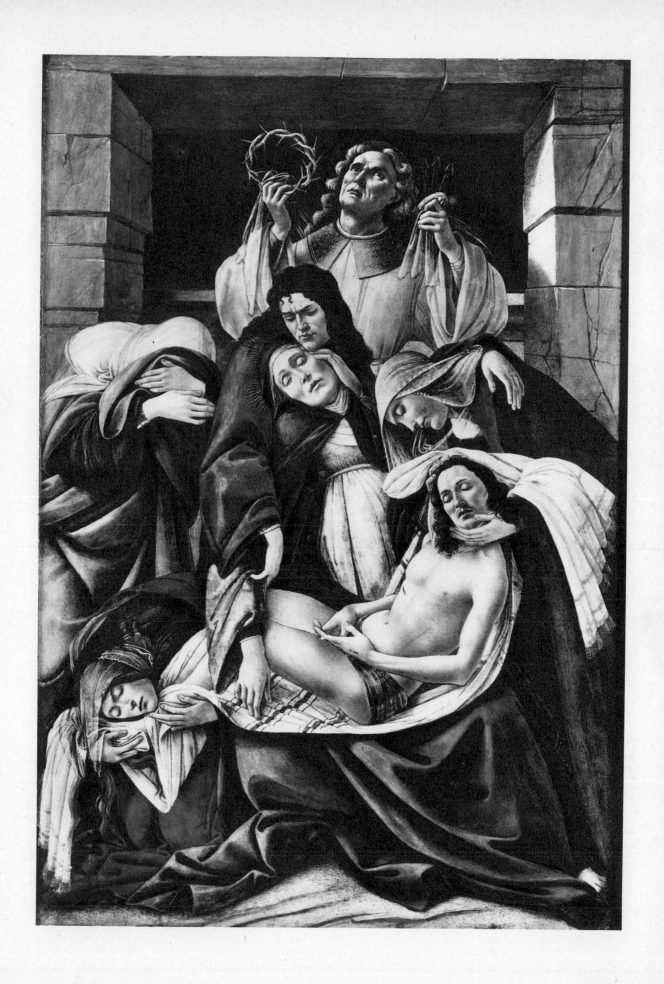

45

SANDRO BOTTICELLI

Pietà
Poldi-Pezzoli Museum, Milan.

46

FILIPPINO LIPPI

The Virgin adoring the Infant Jesus
Galleria degli Uffizi, Florence.

47

FILIPPINO LIPPI

Death of the Centaur
Christ Church College, Oxford.

48

PIERO DI COSIMO

Death of Procris
National Gallery, London.

49

PIERO DI COSIMO

Portrait of Francesco Giamberti
Mauritshuis, The Hague.

50

SASSETTA

St. Anthony Abbott devoting himself to
the Service of God
Kaiser Friedrich Museum, Berlin.

51

SASSETTA

The Marriage of St. Francis with Poverty,
Chastity and Obedience
Musée Condé, Chantilly.

52

GIOVANNI DI PAOLO

St. John the Baptist in the Wilderness
Martin A. Ryerson Collection, Chicago.

53

GENTILE DA FABRIANO

Adoration of the Magi
1423
Galleria degli Uffizi, Florence.

54

GENTILE DA FABRIANO

The Virgin and Child
Yale University, New Haven.

55

PIERO DELLA FRANCESCA

Resurrection
Museo Civico, Borgo San Sepolcro

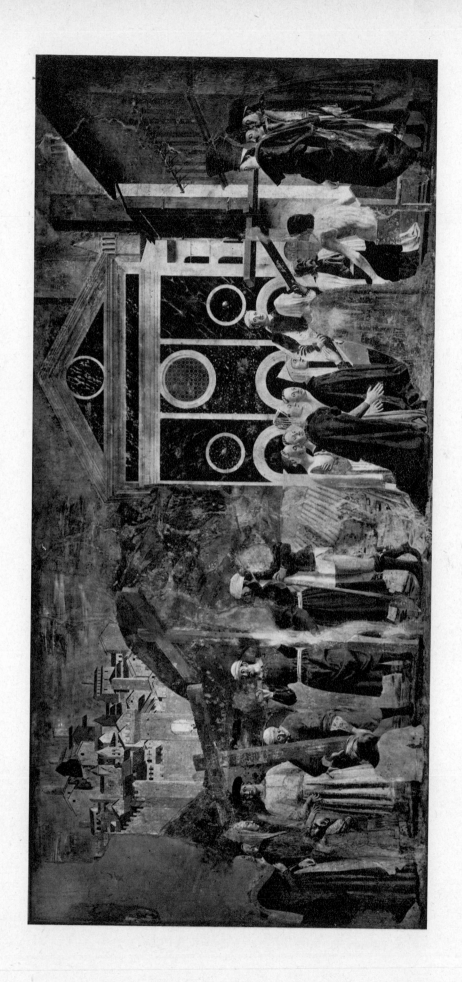

56

PIERO DELLA FRANCESCA

The Empress Helen finding the True Cross.
Chapel of the Choir of S. Francesco, Arezzo.

57

PIERO DELLA FRANCESCA

Flagellation
Ducal Palace, Urbino.

58

PIERO DELLA FRANCESCA

Portrait of Federigo da Montefeltro, Duke
of Urbino
Galleria degli Uffizi, Florence.

59

PIERO DELLA FRANCESCA

Nativity
National Gallery, London.

TEMPLA DOMVM EXPOSITIS:VICOS FORA MOENIA PONTES:
VIRGINEAM TRIVII QVOD REPARARIS AQVAM.
PRISCA LICET NAVTIS STATVAS DARE COMMODA PORTVS:
ET VATICANVM CINGERE SIXTE IVGVM:
PLVS TAMEN VRBS DEBET:NAM QVAE SQVALORE LATEBAT:
CERNITVR IN CELEBRI BIBLIOTHECA LOCO.

60

MELOZZO DA FORLI

Sixtus IV and his Court
1477
Vatican, Pinacoteca, Rome.

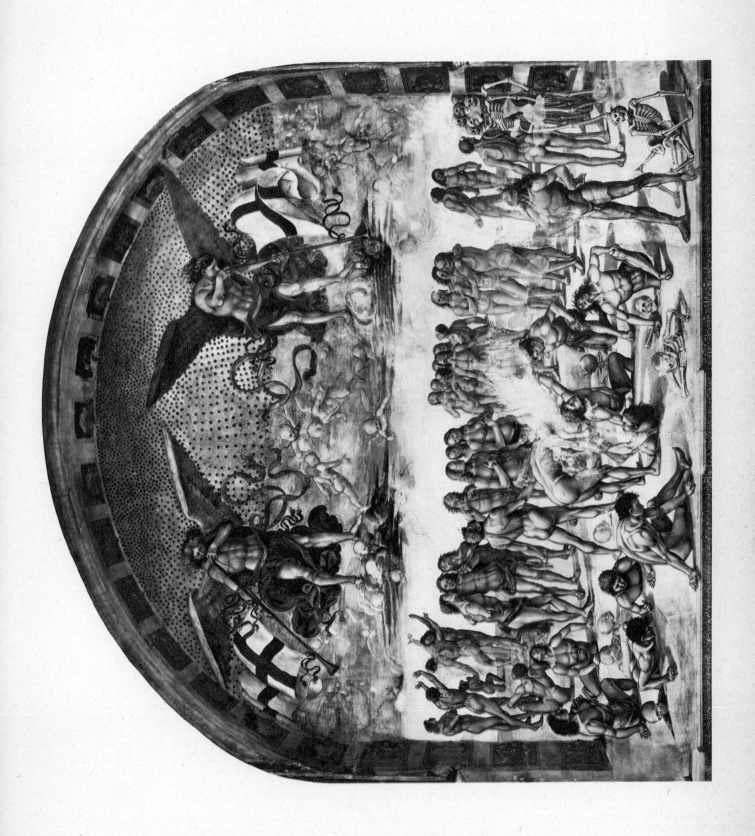

61

LUCA SIGNORELLI

The Last Judgment
Cappella di S. Brizio, Orvieto.

62

LUCA SIGNORELLI

Pan and the Gods
Kaiser Friedrich Museum, Berlin.

63

UMBRIAN MASTER
1473

The Miracle of St. Bernardino
Royal Pinacoteca, Perugia.

64

PERUGINO

The Vision of St. Bernard
1489
Ältere Pinakothek, Munich.

65

BERNARDINO PINTURICCHIO

The Return of Ulysses
National Gallery, London.

66

STEFANO DA VERONA

Madonna in Rose Garden
Museo Civico, Verona.

V

PISANELLO

Profile of Ginevra d'Este
Musée du Louvre, Paris.

67

PISANELLO

Madonna appearing to St. George and
St. Anthony Abbott
National Gallery, London.

68

MICHELE GIAMBONO

San Crisogono
S. Trovaso, Venice.

69

JACOPO BELLINI

Madonna
Galleria Zadini, Lovere.

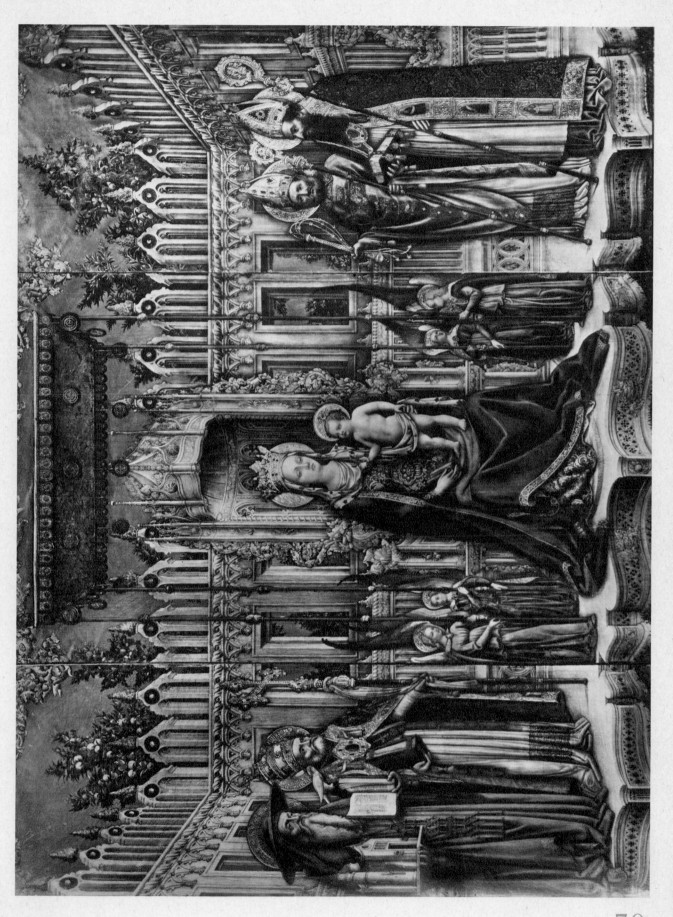

70

ANTONIO VIVARINI and GIOVANNI
D'ALEMAGNA

Madonna Enthroned with four Church
   Fathers
1446
Royal Academy, Venice.

71

BARTOLOMEO VIVARINI

St. George and the Dragon
1485
Kaiser Friedrich Museum, Berlin.

72

ANDREA MANTEGNA

The Martyrdom of St. James
1457
Ovetari Chapel, Eremitani, Padua.

73

ANDREA MANTEGNA

Madonna and Child
Kaiser Friedrich Museum, Berlin.

ANDREA MANTEGNA

Portrait of Federigo Gonzaga with his
Family (detail)
1474
Castello di Corte, Mantua.

VI

ANDREA MANTEGNA

St. Sebastian
Musée du Louvre, Paris.

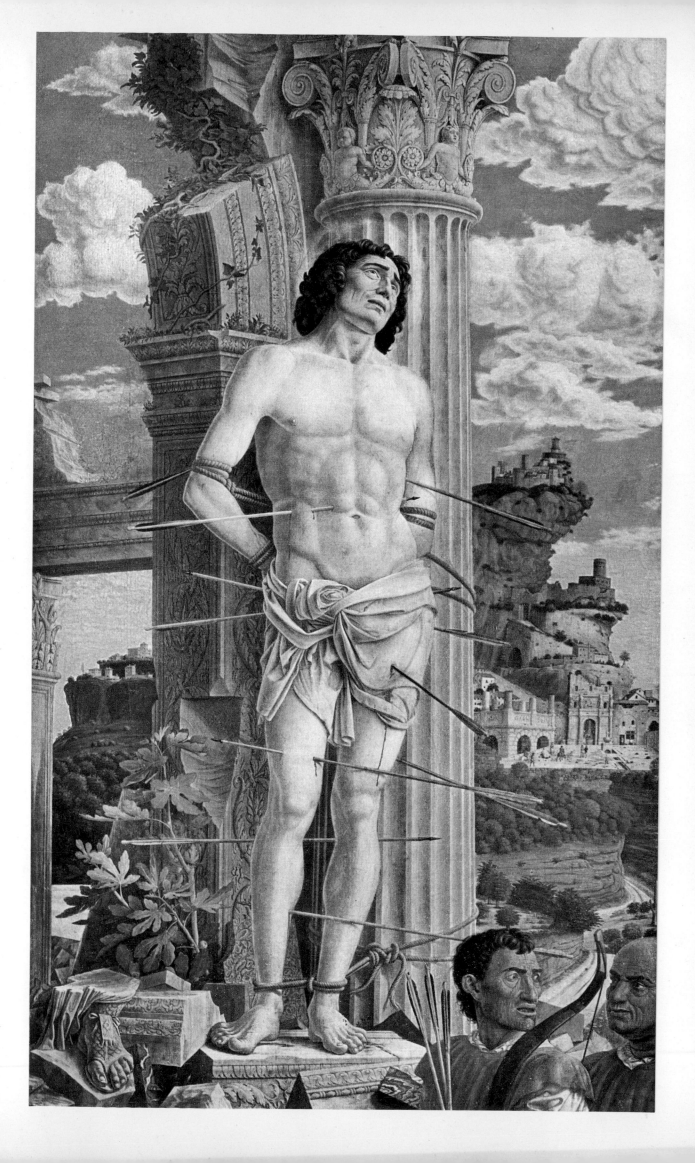

75

GENTILE BELLINI
Portrait of Catherine Cornaro, Queen of
Cyprus
Museum of Fine Arts, Budapest.

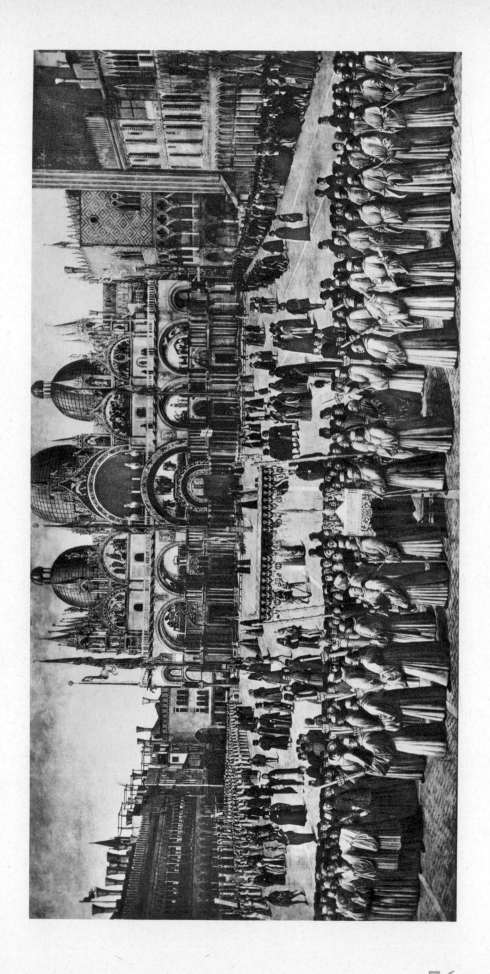

76

GENTILE BELLINI

Corpus Christi Procession
1496
Royal Academy, Venice.

77

VITTORE CARPACCIO

St. Ursula and the Prince take leave of
  their Parents
1495
Royal Academy, Venice.

78

VITTORE CARPACCIO

Portrait of a Young Knight
Schloss Rohoncz, Lugano.

VII

VITTORE CARPACCIO

St. Stephen preaching in Jerusalem
1511-1520
Musée du Louvre, Paris.

79

CARLO CRIVELLI

Annunciation
1486
National Gallery, London.

80

COSIMO TURA

Pietà
Museo Civico Correr, Venice.

81

COSIMO TURA

The Blessed Jacopo della Marca
1484
Galleria Estense, Modena.

82

FERRARESE MASTER

circa 1460
Autumn
Kaiser Friedrich Museum, Berlin.

83

FERRARESE MASTER

circa 1480
Portrait of Uberto de' Sacrati and his
    Family
Ältere Pinakothek, Munich.

84

ERCOLE DE' ROBERTI

St. John the Baptist
Kaiser Friedrich Museum, Berlin.

85

ERCOLE DE ROBERTI

The Argonauts approaching Colchis
Museo Civiso, Padua.

86

LORENZO COSTA

Portrait presumed to be of Eleonore
Gonzaga
Hampton Court Palace.

87

ANTONELLO DA MESSINA

The Virgin of the Annunciation
Museo Nazionale, Palermo.

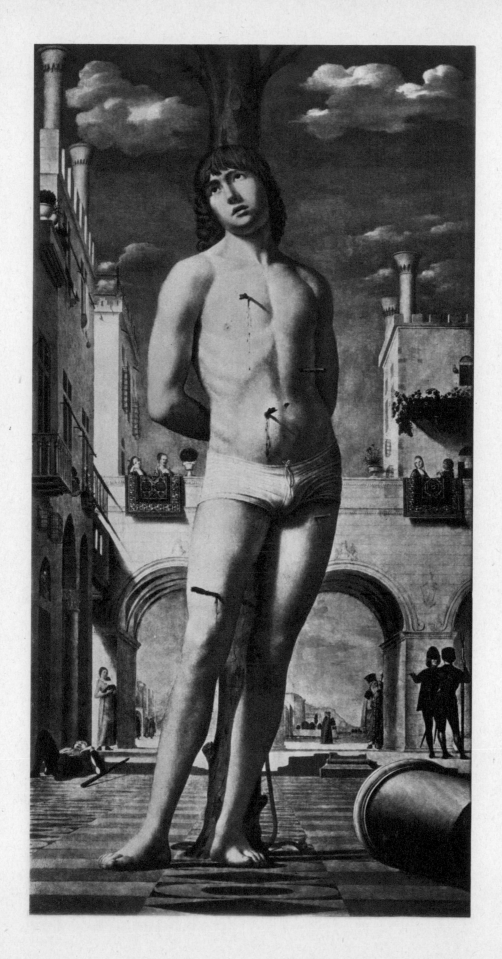

88

ANTONELLO DA MESSINA

St. Sebastian
1476
Gemäldegalerie, Dresden.

VIII

ANTONELLO DA MESSINA

Il Condottiere
1475
Musée du Louvre, Paris.

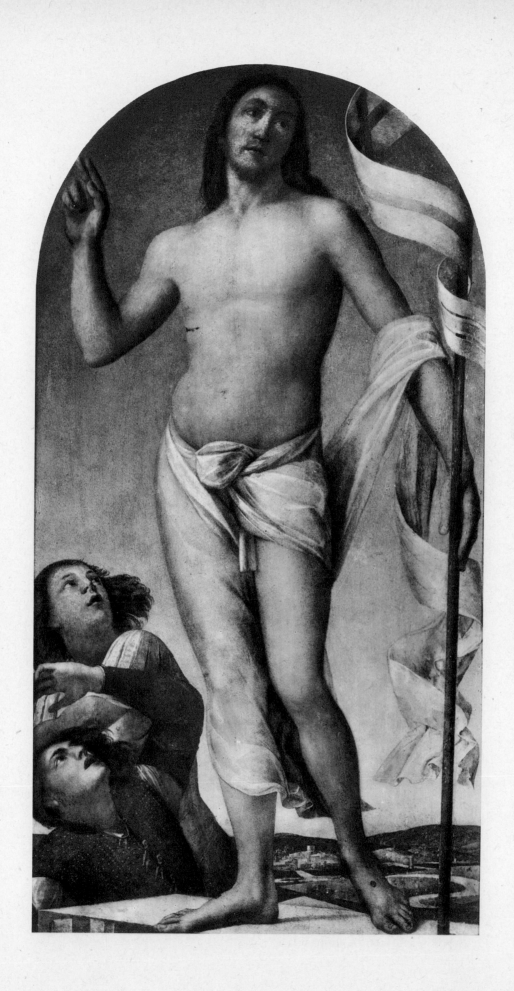

89

ALVISE VIVARINI

Resurrection
San Giovanni in Bragora, Venice.

90

BARTOLOMMEO MONTAGNA

Pietà with St. Joseph, St. John and Mary-
Magdalen
Monte Berico, Sanctuary, Vicenza.

91

CIMA DA CONEGLIANO

Baptism
1494
High Altar of San Giovanni in Bragora,
Venice.

92

CIMA DA CONEGLIANO

Endymion and Selene
Royal Gallry, Parma.

93

GIOVANNI BELLINI

The Dead Christ supported by Angels
Palazzo Communale, Rimini.

94

GIOVANNI BELLINI

Transfiguration
Museo Nazionale, Naples.

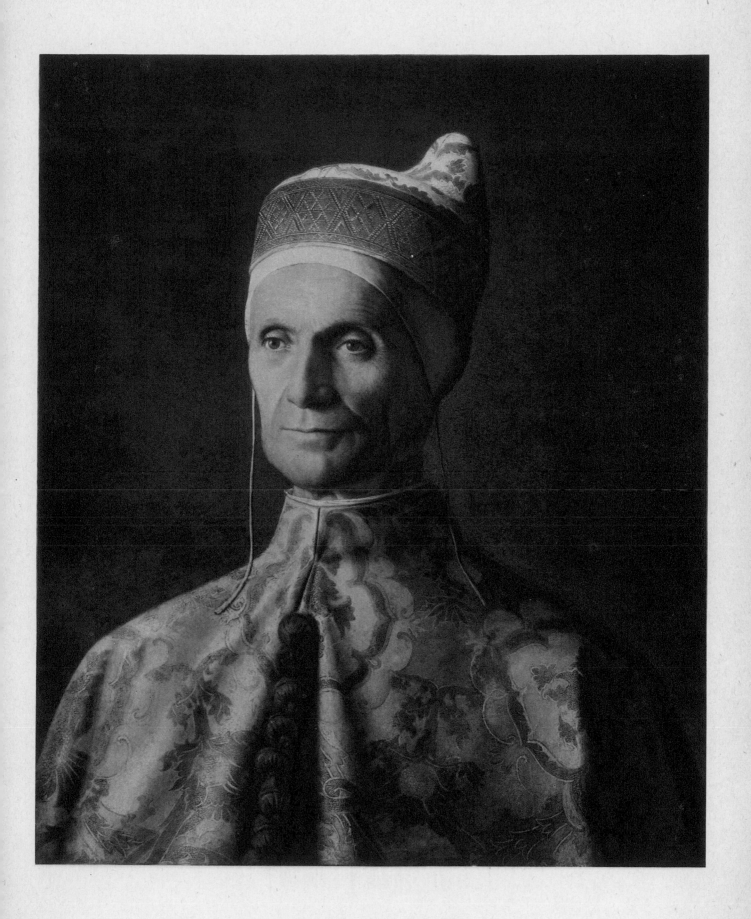

95

GIOVANNI BELLINI

Doge Loredan (detail)
National Gallery, London.

96

GIOVANNI BELLINI

Feast of the Gods
1514
Widener Collection, Philadelphia.